FOUR Y
of
SWAMI VIVEKANANDA

Condensed and retold by

SWAMI TAPASYANANDA

Advaita Ashrama
(PUBLICATION DEPARTMENT)
5 DEHI ENTALLY ROAD · KOLKATA 700 014

Published by
Swami Tattwavidananda
Adhyaksha, Advaita Ashrama
Mayavati, Champawat, Uttarakhand, Himalayas
from its Publication Department, Kolkata
Email : mail@advaitaashrama.org
Website : www.advaitaashrama.org

First Edition, September 1979
Second Edition, 1983
Third Edition, 1987
Fourth Edition, July 2013
First Reprint, December 2015
3M3C

ISBN 978-81-7505-089-1

Printed in India at
Trio Process
Kolkata 700 014

PUBLISHER'S NOTE

One may pertinently ask, 'Where is the need for this book, when the four well-known *yogas* of Swami Vivekananda are available in English in a comprehensive form?' A satisfactory answer to this question is found in the 'Preface' written by Swami Tapasyananda, who has 'condensed and retold' the four *yogas* of Swamiji in an easily readable style.

This book has already undergone two editions in 1979 and 1983, both published by Sri Ramakrishna Math, Mylapore, Madras, indicating its popularity among the admirers and followers of the great Swami. The copyright of the book has since been made over to Advaita Ashrama, Mayavati. In publishing this third edition, we wish to express our profound gratitude to Sri Ramakrishna Math, Mylapore, Madras.

1 May 1987   PUBLISHER
Advaita Ashrama
Mayavati, Himalayas

PREFACE

This volume of about two hundred and fifty pages dealing with the four yogas—karma yoga, raja yoga, bhakti yoga and jnana yoga—is a *precis* of Swami Vivekananda's great lectures on these subjects published originally in four volumes, here condensed into about one third of the original. Attempt has been made here to compress the matter both by abridgement and re-telling, while at the same time retaining several inspiring passages of the original, which are put in quotations.

The object of this book is two-fold—on the one hand, to help new students of Swami Vivekananda literature with a general survey of the teachings which they are going to study in detail in the original, and on the other hand, to give those who have already studied them in the original, a brief Note to help refresh their memory. Every effort has been made to be very faithful to the original, as also to interest the reader in the original speeches of the great Swami through their summarised presentation, interspersed with appropriate quotations.

The main features of the book are: 1. It compresses the matter into a little less than one third of the original.

2. The subject of each chapter is thoroughly analysed and topical subsidiary headings are given. 3. With the exception of jnana yoga, summaries of the other yogas are given at the end of each book. 4. In the raja yoga, the second part comprises the *Yoga Aphorisms* and the comments on them. Here the *Aphorisms* are omitted. The comments are summarised under appropriate sub-headings, which have reference to the Sutras.

There is also another purpose behind this abridgement. It is the experience of many readers of Swami Vivekananda literature that they are not able to grasp the thought content of them, though it elates them and grips their attention. If we analyze the reason for this, it will be found in the nature of the Text itself. They are of such a high inspirational quality and are so highly charged with emotion that they become more a subject of experience than an object of analytical thought. Not that there are not thoughts and well-packed arguments on recondite topics in them, but the brilliance of the inspirational quality keeps the other excellences submerged. Men therefore are inclined to read them more with their hearts than their head. One object of the abridgement and retelling is to lift up and hold to view the rich thought content, which some at least might have missed in their reading of the original.

If this condensed version of the yogas in this series called 'Studies in Swami Vivekananda' is successful

and meets the need of students of Swami Vivekananda
literature, we shall follow it up with two other similar
volumes on 'The Other Philosophic Lectures of Swami
Vivekananda' and 'The Nationalistic Lectures of Swami
Vivekananda.'

Sri Ramakrishna Math
Madras   PUBLISHER
1.11.1979

CONTENTS

PART 3: BHAKTI YOGA

Section 1: Apara-bhakti or Preparatory Devotion

PART 1: KARMA YOGA

1
EFFECT OF KARMA ON CHARACTER

1.1 KNOWLEDGE AS THE GOAL OF LIFE

Knowledge is the goal of mankind, not pleasure, as man mistakenly thinks. Pleasure and pain, happiness and suffering are our teachers. Through their impact on the mind, character develops. Often it is suffering that helps the development of character more than happiness. It acts as a friction that brings out the inner fire.

All knowledge is inherent in man. It does not come from outside. All external factors are only stimulations that help its manifestation. 'Like fire in a piece of flint, knowledge exists in the mind'. Work, with its consequences of enjoyments and sufferings, is the friction that brings it out. Every mental and physical activity is like a blow administered to the soul, by which fire is struck, as it were, from it, and its power and knowledge are made to manifest. This is the nature and function of karma in its widest sense.

1.2 KARMA AND CHARACTER FORMATION

Just as a large number of small waves create a big wave, the effects of karma accumulate to form tendencies, an aggregation of which in a personality we call character. Man is like a centre attracting all the powers of the universe towards himself, fusing them all together and sending out his inner reaction to them as a current—the manifestation of his will, which in common parlance we call his personality or character. The mightiest of such waves of character are the Buddhas and the Christs of the world. They are the products of several lives of accumulation of tendencies born of work, Now 'Work for work's sake' is the most potent factor in the generation of tremendous characters like that of the Buddha and the Christ—'gigantic souls, with wills powerful enough to overturn worlds, wills they got by persistent work, through ages, and ages.' Ordinarily, people work only for selfish gains in this world or the hereafter, or for reputation, or as expiation for sins committed. In such works the moral energy of action is frittered away while there may be worldly gains accruing. But unselfish work, done merely because one believes in doing good and loves good, goes to the conservation of will and moral energy, and generates mighty characters. 'All outgoing energy following a selfish motive is frittered away; it will not cause power to return to you; but if restrained, it will result in development of power. This self-control will tend to produce a mighty will, a character which makes a Christ or a Buddha.' 'Unselfishness is more paying, only people have not the patience to practise it. ... Love, truth, and unselfishness are not merely moral figures of speech, but they form our highest ideals, because in them lies such a manifestation of power.' These will make men into moral giants; only they will have to wait for the accumulation of these tendencies.

1.3 THE TRUE NATURE OF INWARDNESS

A question will be raised here—what is the place in this scheme of spiritual discipline for quietness, solitude and inwardness, which are associated with spiritual development? The answer is that man must learn to find solitude in the midst of work. 'The ideal man is he who, in the midst of the greatest silence and solitude, finds the intensest activity, and in the midst of the intensest activity finds the silence and solitude of the desert. ... He goes through the streets of a big city with all its traffic, and his mind is as calm as if he were in a cave, where not a sound could reach him; and he is intensely working all the time. That is the ideal of Karma-Yoga, and if you have attained to that you have really learnt the secret of work.'

2

EACH IS GREAT IN HIS OWN PLACE

2.1 KARMA YOGA AS A SCHEME
OF GRADUAL GROWTH

This sublime ideal of karma yoga should not be taught or taken as a discouragement or condemnation of men who cannot rise up to it: 'Even the lowest forms of work are not to be despised. Let the man, who knows no better, work for selfish ends, for name and fame; but everyone should always try to get towards higher and higher motives and to understand them.'

Another such sublime ideal is the teaching, 'Resist not evil.' (That is, do not react with hatred and violence against forces that oppose you.) Before this teaching becomes applicable, man must have the power to resist. Without that, non-resistance will only be an act of cowardice. The law for such a person is first to develop that power of resistance, be it even through its use at first, and after he has secured the power, to put the higher discipline into practice. For, duty and morality vary for individuals according to their mental constitution. Their

capacity is determined by the stage or level of their evolution. What is relevant to him immediately is the next
stage of evolution and not what is ultimate. Without
recognising this, to harp only on the ultimate will be
'equivalent to condemning a vast portion of mankind.
Not only so, it would be making men feel that they
were always doing wrong, and cause in them scruples
of conscience in all their actions; it would weaken them,
and that constant self-disapproval would breed more
vice than any other weakness would. To the man who
has begun to hate himself the gate to degeneration has
already opened; and the same is true of a nation.'

The constitution of the body and the mind of man
is based upon the three forces of nature—sattva, rajas
and tamas—which stand for balance, activity and inert-
ness. Man's character and his eligibility for particular
moral standards depend on the relative dominance of
these forces in him. The ancient Hindu scheme of life
based on four *ashrams* and four *varnas* was based on the
recognition of this principle. Its aim was to give, while
placing the highest ideal before man, also adaptations
of it for men of different natures and different stages of
evolution—a practical way to evolve to higher standards
through graded codes of conduct and activity. 'To each
of these stages of life certain duties are attached. No one
of these stages is intrinsically superior to another. The
life of the married man is quite as great as that of the

celibate who has devoted himself to religious work. The
scavenger in the street is quite as great and glorious as
the king on his throne. Take him off his throne, make
him do the work of the scavenger, and see how he fares.
Take up the scavenger and see how he will rule. It is
useless to say that the man who lives out of the world is
a greater man than he who lives in the world; it is much
more difficult to live in the world and worship God than
to give it up and live a free and easy life.'

'If a man retires from the world to worship God, he
must not think that those who live in the world and
work for the good of the world are not worshipping
God: neither must those who live in the world, for wife
and children, think that those who give up the world
are low vagabonds. Each is great in his own place'—as
the following story illustrates:

2.2 HOUSEHOLDER OR *SANNYASIN*— WHO IS GREATER?

A king was always in the habit of questioning
scholars and holy men: who is greater, a *sannyasin* or a
householder? He wanted valid reasons also for the view
expressed. No one was able to give him a satisfactory
answer. At last a good *sannyasin* visited the king. When
the point at issue was referred to him, he said that each
is equally great in his place, and offered to prove it, if

the king followed him in his wanderings for a few days. Agreeing to this proposal, the king set out with the *sannyasin*. In the course of their travel, they reached a place where the ruling monarch had arranged a *swayamvara* (marriage by choice) for his daughter. In a *swayamvara* the girl chooses from among the assembled suitors the one she likes best. The king had proclaimed also that he would give half his kingdom to the man whom his daughter chose. So a large number of princes had assembled; but the girl, instead of choosing any of them, put the ceremonial garland of choice on a young and handsome *sannyasin* who was watching the scene from a corner. Startled at it, the *sannyasin* threw the garland away and walked fast from the place, followed by the girl who was madly infatuated with him. Towards evening, the *sannyasin* entered a forest and disappeared into the woods. While the girl was standing stranded in the forest, not knowing where to go, the king and the first *sannyasin*, who were following the two, went to her help. All the three of them took shelter under a tree on that cold night. A small bird, its mate and children saw from their nest these people shivering from cold under the tree. As a householder, the bird thought it its duty to extend them hospitality. It flew away, got a bit of burning firewood in its beak, and dropped it to its guests, who made a fire with it and relieved themselves of the cold. Next the bird thought it its duty to give some food to these hungry guests, and threw itself into the fire glowing below, so that they might eat its burnt flesh. Now its wife felt that one small bird would be insufficient for three, and so threw herself also into the fire in pursuance of the wifely duty of fulfilling the purpose of the dead husband. The parents' footsteps were followed by the children too, as they felt it was their duty to carry on the work of their parents. Thus all of them courted death in the discharge of their duties.

The *sannyasin* then said to the king who was surprised by all the experiences he had that day: 'King, you have seen that each is great in his own place. If you want to live in the world, live like those birds, ready at any moment to sacrifice yourself for others. If you want to renounce the world, be like that young man to whom the most beautiful woman and a kingdom were as nothing. If you want to be a householder, hold your life a sacrifice for the welfare of others; and if you choose the life of renunciation, do not even look at beauty and money and power. Each is great in his own place, but the duty of the one is not the duty of the other.'

3

DETACHED WORK: ITS SECRET

3.1 THE PROBLEM OF GOOD AND EVIL INVOLVED IN WORK

To feed the hungry, to cure the sick, to educate a man so that he may stand on his own feet—these are all good and valuable forms of service. But spiritual service which gives enlightenment to man, which makes him strong, which removes all his wants for ever, is the highest form of service.

All work is a mixture of good and evil in its results. Both good and bad deeds produce their Karmic effects and bind the doer. The teaching of the *Gita* for solving this problem is that if the doer does not attach himself to the work, its results do not affect him.

All work leaves an effect on the mind of man. It is their cumulative effect on the mind that expresses itself as character. When a man has been repeatedly and continuously doing good and avoiding evil, good action will become automatic with him. His character gets established in goodness, and he develops the capacity to control and restrain his senses and the mind if they drag him in the wrong direction.

3.2 THE IDEAL OF WORKING IN FREEDOM

There is, however, a still higher stage of work in which there is not even the bondage of the good. It is the ideal of working in complete freedom. This is what the Gita teaches as detached work. To be detached there are two requirements: (1) We have to be established in the idea that this world is not our real habitation, but only one of the many stages through which we are passing. Man in his ignorance thinks that the soul is for nature. But the truth is that nature is for the soul, for its education and ultimate liberation. When we regard ourselves as part of nature and its qualities, we are bound by the impressions that experiences generate. We become slaves. (2) Freedom is possible only through love, and not through the slavery that attachments produce. All attached work is only slave's work. It is not based on true love, for there is no love in slavery. The test of love is this: 'Every act of love brings happiness; there is no act of love which does not bring peace and blessedness as its reaction. Real existence, real knowledge, and real love are eternally connected with one another, the three in one: where one of them is, the others also must be; they are the three aspects of the One without a second' 'Krishna says, "Look at Me, Arjuna! If I stop from work for one moment, the whole universe will die. I have nothing to gain from work; I am the one Lord, but why do I work? Because I love the world." God is unattached because He loves; that real love makes us unattached. Wherever there is attachment, the clinging to the things of the world, you must know that it is all physical attraction between sets of particles of matter—something that attracts two bodies nearer and nearer all the time and, if they cannot get near enough, produces pain; but where there is real love, it does not rest on physical attachment at all. Such lovers may be a thousand miles away from one another, but their love will be all the same. ... If you can invariably take the position of a giver, in which everything given by you is a free offering to the world, without any thought of return, then will your work bring you no attachment. Attachment comes only where we expect a return.'

People often talk of 'rights and justice'. In fact what guides the conduct of man is only 'might or mercy'— might standing for all that is selfish, and mercy for all that is divine.

According to the path of devotion, unattached work takes another form. It consists in looking upon all work as 'worship' in case we believe in a personal God. Here we offer all the fruits of our work to Him, and therefore we have no right to expect any return for it from mankind. The Lord Himself works incessantly and is ever without attachment. Just as water cannot wet the lotus leaf, so work cannot bind the unselfish man having no attachment to results. 'The selfless and unattached man may live in the very heart of a crowded and sinful city; he will not be touched by sin.'

3.4 AN EXAMPLE OF UNSELFISH WORK

The Mahabharata gives the following story of un-selfish work. After the Mahabharata war, the Pandava brothers performed a great sacrifice, in which gifts without limit were distributed among holy men and the poor. A mongoose with half of his body golden in colour was found rolling on the floor of the hall where gifts were being distributed. On being asked the reason, he declared: 'You are all liars; this is no sacrifice. ... There was once a little village, and in it there dwelt a poor Brahmin with his wife, his son, and his son's wife ... There came in that land a three years' famine, and the poor Brahmin suffered more than ever. At last when the family had starved for days, the father brought home one morning a little barley flour (which) ... he divided it into four parts, one for each member of the family. They prepared it for their meal, and just as they were about to eat, there was a knock at the door. ... and there stood a guest. ... So the poor Brahmin said, "Come in, sir; you

are welcome," He set before the guest his own portion of
the food, which the guest quickly ate and said, "Oh, sir,
you have killed me; I have been starving for ten days,
and this little bit has but increased my hunger." Then
the wife said to her husband, "Give him my share," but
the husband said, "Not so." The wife however insisted,
saying, "Here is a poor man, and it is our duty as house-
holders to see that he is fed, and it is my duty as a wife
to give him my portion, seeing that you have no more to
offer him." Then she gave her share to the guest, which
he ate, and said he was still burning with hunger. So
the son said, "Take my portion also; it is the duty of a
son to help his father to fulfil his obligations." The guest
ate that, but remained still unsatisfied; so the son's wife
gave him her portion also. That was sufficient, and the
guest departed, blessing them. That night those four
people died of starvation. A few granules of that flour
had fallen on the floor; and when I rolled my body on
them, half of it became golden, as you see. Since then I
have been travelling all over the world, hoping to find
another sacrifice like that, but nowhere have I found
one; nowhere else has the other half of my body been
turned into gold. That is why I say this is no sacrifice.
Karma yoga therefore means helping others even to the
point of death, without asking for any return. 'Never
vaunt of your gifts to the poor or expect their gratitude,
but rather be grateful to them for giving you the occa-

sion of practicing charity to them. Thus it is plain that to be an ideal householder is a much more difficult task than to be an ideal Sannyasin; the true life of work is indeed as hard as, if not harder than, the equally true life of renunciation.'

4

CONCEPT OF DUTY

4.1 DEFINITION OF DUTY

In the study of karma yoga it is necessary to know what is meant by the concept of duty. The difficulty is that there is no uniform and universally accepted norm in regard to it. It varies from community to community, country to country, time to time, situation to situation, one state of life to another. The ordinary idea of duty everywhere is that every good man follows the dictates of his conscience. But what is it that makes an act a duty? If a Christian finds a piece of beef before him and does not eat it to save his own life, or will not give it to save the life of another man, he is sure to feel that he has not done his duty. But if a Hindu dares to eat that piece of beef or to give it to another Hindu, he is equally sure to feel that he too has not done his duty; the Hindu's training and education make him feel that way. In the last century there were notorious bands of robbers in India called thugs; they thought it their duty to kill any man they could and take away his money; the larger the number of men they killed, the better they thought they were. Ordinarily if a man goes out into the street and shoots down another man, he is apt to feel sorry for it, thinking that he has done wrong. But if the very same man, as a soldier in his regiment, kills not one but twenty, he is certain to feel glad and think that he has done his duty remarkably well. Therefore we see that it is not the thing done that defines a duty. To give an objective definition of duty is thus entirely impossible. Yet there is duty from the subjective side. Any action that makes us go Godward is a good action, and is our duty; any action that makes us go downward is evil, and is not our duty. From the subjective standpoint we may see that certain acts have a tendency to exalt and ennoble us, while certain other acts have a tendency to degrade and to brutalise us. But it is not possible to make out with certainty which acts have which kind of tendency in relation to all persons, of all sorts and conditions.'

4.2 DUTY AND UNSELFISHNESS

'The Bhagavad-Gita frequently alludes to duties dependent upon birth and position in life. Birth and position in life and in society largely determine the mental and moral attitude of individuals towards the various activities of life. It is therefore our duty to do that work which will exalt and ennoble us in accordance with the ideals and activities of the society in which we are born.' But it must be particularly remembered that the same ideals will not prevail in all societies and even in one society at all times. Forgetfulness of this leads to fanaticism, intolerance and brutality in the name of ideals.

'Yet it is work through the sense of duty that leads us to work without any idea of duty; when work will become worship—nay, something higher—then will work be done for its own sake. We shall find that the philosophy of duty, whether it be in the form of ethics or of love, is the same as in every other Yoga—the object being the attenuating of the lower self, so that the real higher Self may shine forth—the lessening of the frittering away of energies on the lower plane of existence, so that the soul may manifest itself on the higher ones. This is accomplished by the continuous denial of low desires, which duty rigorously requires. The whole organisation of society has thus been developed, consciously or unconsciously, in the realms of action and experience, where, by limiting selfishness, we open the way to an unlimited expansion of the real nature of man.'

4.3 DUTY AND LOVE

'Duty is seldom sweet. It is only when love greases its wheels that it runs smoothly. ... and love shines in freedom alone. ... the highest expression of freedom is to forbear.' In the fulfilment of domestic duties in life, disharmony arises because the relationships are established not on love based on freedom, but on attachment based on selfishness.

'Chastity is the first virtue in man or woman, and the man who, however he may have strayed away, cannot be brought to the right path by a gentle and loving and chaste wife is indeed very rare.' A good, chaste wife, who thinks of every other man except her own husband as her child and has an attitude of a mother towards all men, will grow so great in the power of her purity that there cannot be a single man, however brutal, who will not breathe an atmosphere of holiness in her presence. Similarly every husband must look upon all women, except his own wife, as mother, sister or daughter. The man again, who wants to be a teacher of religion, must look upon every woman as his mother, and always behave towards her as such.

'It is the duty of the mother to think of her children first and then of herself. But, instead of that, if the parents are always thinking of themselves first, the result is that the relation between parents and children becomes the same as that between birds and their offspring which, as soon as they are fledged, do not recognise any parents. Blessed, indeed, is the man who is able to look upon woman as the representative of the

motherhood of God. Blessed, indeed, is the woman to
whom man represents the fatherhood of God. Blessed
are the children who look upon their parents as Divinity manifested on earth.'

The Mahabharata has an instructive story to illustrate
how discharge of duties through pure, disinterested
love can take man to the highest spiritual eminence. An
ascetic with some psychic powers once went for *biksha*
(alms) to a house. He was, however, kept waiting for
some time by the housewife, who was engaged in her
household duties. Full of anger at the delay, the ascetic
thought of his miraculous power by which he had burnt
with a mere look a crow and a crane that caused disturbance to his meditation by their cries. After some time the
housewife cried out to the surprise of the ascetic, mildly
chiding him, saying that all were not crow and crane,
to be burnt in the flame of his anger. Surprised at the
woman's awareness of a fact which was, in the nature
of things, absolutely unknown to any, the ascetic asked
her how she had developed such powers of mind, and
got the reply that it was by discharging her duties as
housewife without any selfish motives that she had had
her mental development. She also advised him to go to
a neighbouring butcher, if he wanted to know more of
how a man can develop by doing his duties properly.
It was the greatest surprise of his life to be told that he
would have to learn wisdom from a butcher, of all men.

But it was a still greater surprise when he understood
that this butcher at his gruesome work had already come
to know by intuition who had sent him to his shop. The
butcher asked him to wait for some time, and after he
had finished his work, took him home with him. Then
he attended to the needs of his sick and old parents and
afterwards came to converse with the ascetic. To some
questions of the ascetic on themes like God and the
soul, he gave a learned and enlightening talk, which
is called 'Vyadha Gita' in the *Mahabharata*. Mystified
by all these unexpected experiences, the ascetic asked
him why, in spite of his great wisdom, he was doing
this gruesome work of a butcher. The butcher replied:
'My son,' replied the Vyadha, "no duty is ugly, no duty
is impure. My birth placed me in these circumstances
and environments. In my boyhood I learnt the trade;
I am unattached, and I try to do my duty well. I try to
do my duty as a householder, and I try to do all I can to
make my father and mother happy. I neither know your
Yoga, nor have I become a Sannyasin, nor did I go out
of the world into a forest; nevertheless, all that you have
heard and seen has come to me through the unattached
doing of the duty which belongs to my position.' "

'... a great Yogi. ... told me once the secret of work,
"Let the end and the means be joined into one." When
you are doing any work, do not think of anything beyond. Do it as worship, as the highest worship, and

devote your whole life to it for the time being. Thus in the story, the Vyadha and the woman did their duty with cheerfulness and whole-heartedness, and the result was that they became *illuminated*, clearly showing that the right performance of the duties of any station in life, without attachment to results, leads us to the highest realisation of the perfection of the soul. It is the worker who is attached to results that grumbles about the nature of the duty which has fallen to his lot; to the unattached worker all duties are equally good, and form efficient instruments with which selfishness and sensuality may be killed, and the freedom of the soul secured. We are all apt to think too highly of ourselves. Our duties are determined by our deserts to a much larger extent than we are willing to grant. Competition rouses envy, and it kills the kindliness of the heart. To the grumbler all duties are distasteful; nothing will ever satisfy him, and his whole life is doomed to prove a failure. Let us work on, doing as we go whatever happens to be our duty, and being ever ready to put our shoulders to the wheel. Then surely shall we see the Light!'

5

IN HELPING THE WORLD
WE HELP OURSELVES

5.1 RITUALS AND SYMBOLISM

Besides the topic of duty, karma yoga includes also those aspects of religion known as ritualism and symbolism. It is the average man's incapacity to grasp abstract ideas that has made rituals and symbols necessary. In a sense the whole universe is a symbol pointing towards God, who is its essence. Many of the great symbols are universal and cannot be traced to any human origin. Thus the cross, the swastika, the circle, etc., have appeared in different cultures. They must have developed independently in these various cultures, as these cultures are separated from one another by vast distances in space and time. Symbols may be sound symbols and colour symbols also. Even words are symbols of ideas. There has never been an idea without a word, and a word without an idea. They are inseparable. Words are a force, and they play a decisive role in the life of man. 'The external aspect of the thought of God is the

Word, and as God thought and willed before He created, creation came out of the Word.' Language is not
the result of a convention—of some people agreeing to
represent certain ideas by certain words. Symbols too
are natural growths in the same way. It is therefore impossible to create by convention a system of symbols
as in the case of a language. Many say today there is
no use for temples and rituals. That is a wrong way of
thinking. The association of particular temples, rituals
and other concrete forms with particular religions has
a tendency to bring into the mind of the followers of
those religions, the thought for which these concrete
forms stand as symbols, just as the words of a language
bring the corresponding thought to the minds of the
people who speak it. It is not wise to ignore rituals and
symbology altogether.

5.2 BY HELPING OTHERS W˜ ONLY HELP OURSELVES

Helping others and doing good to the world are
fundamental ideas in karma yoga. But a true karma
yogin must understand that through all his work he
can do only very little good to the world. For, the world
we want to improve is too big, and our powers and our
control over it are too limited. The little we do today
can easily be wiped off tomorrow by an earthquake or
a flood or a war. The world is in the hands of a power
higher than ourselves. What is really achieved by doing

good to others is that one improves oneself. 'This world is like a dog's curly tail, and people have been striving to straighten it out for hundreds of years; but when they let it go, it has curled up again.' A jinn was once brought under the control of a man on condition that the man would give him work always. The man thought that he could easily do it, and ordered the jinn to put up buildings, bring money, grow gardens, etc. But soon he found that all his wants were exhausted and he could no longer engage the jinn in any work. The jinn was about to attack and swallow him, when he was advised by a wise friend to give the jinn a dog's tail to straighten as the next piece of work. The jinn started on this new task, but found he could never straighten the tail, however much he might try. Such is the nature of the world and man's effort to improve it. If we know this, we will not become fanatics in our schemes of improving the world. 'You need not worry or make yourself sleepless about the world; it will go on without you. When you have avoided fanaticism, then alone will you work well. It is the level-headed man, the calm man, of good judgement and cool nerves, of great sympathy and love, who does good work and so does good to himself.'

'Yet we must do good; the desire to do good is the highest motive power we have, if we know all the time that it is a privilege to help others. Do not stand on a high pedestal and take five cents in your hand and say,

"Here, my poor man," but be grateful that the poor man is there, so that by making a gift to him you are able to help yourself. It is not the receiver that is blessed, but it is the giver. Be thankful that you are allowed to exercise your power of benevolence and mercy in the world, and thus become pure and perfect.'

5.3 BELIEF IN GOD MAKES KARMA YOGA EASIER

The karma yogin must also know that 'there is a God in this universe. It is not true that this universe is drifting and stands in need of help from you and me. God is ever present therein, He is undying and eternally active and infinitely watchful. When the whole universe sleeps, He sleeps not; He is working incessantly; all the changes and manifestations of the world are His.' If a worker remembers this, he will not be a fanatic or an egoist. True non-attachment is possible only when work is prompted neither by fanaticism nor by expectation of rewards, but out of pure love and humility. In such an attitude, the giver feels blessed that he has got an opportunity to serve. He is not disappointed even if the receiver is not grateful to him, or if his schemes of service are miscarried. He understands the limitations of the world and its affairs, and is always calm and collected. And 'the calmer we are and the less disturbed our nerves, the more shall we love and the better will our work be.'

6

NON-ATTACHMENT IS
SELF-ABNEGATION

6.1 GOOD AND BAD EFFECTS OF WORK: HOW TO
SOLVE THEIR DICHOTOMY

The good and the evil thoughts and actions of men
leave behind them subtle vibrations which remain active
in the moral atmosphere. If a person indulges in bad actions now, he attunes himself to these vibrations of evil
accumulated in the past, and these act upon him and
promote his degeneration all the more. So also a man
who is good opens himself to the beneficial vibrations,
and his tendency to do good gets further strengthened.
'We run, therefore, a twofold danger in doing evil: first,
we open ourselves to all the evil influences surrounding
us; secondly, we create evil which affects others, may
be hundreds of years hence. In doing evil we injure
ourselves and others also.'

Now in determining the goodness and badness of
actions, one difficulty arises. No action can be cent per
cent good or cent per cent bad. All actions are a mixture

of both, though there may be dominance of one or the other in a given action. 'That being the case, it naturally follows that perfection can never be attained by work. We may work through all eternity, but there will be no way out of this intricate maze. You may work on, and on, and on; there will be no end to this inevitable association of good and evil in the results of work.'

This impasse in the moral situation has made some religious sects advocate a theory of suicide by starvation as the highest ideal of life and a way to get over the moral problem of the individual. But the true solution lies in the *Gita* doctrine of non-attachment in work. Non-attachment consists in being unselfish. 'Enjoyment should not be the goal. First kill your self and then take the whole world as yourself; as the old Christians used to say, "The old man must die." This old man is the selfish idea that the whole world is made for our enjoyment. Foolish parents teach their children to pray, "O Lord, Thou hast created this sun for me and this moon for me," as if the Lord has had nothing else to do than to create everything for these babies. Do not teach your children such nonsense. Then again, there are people who are foolish in another way: they teach us that all these animals were created for us to kill and eat, and that this universe is for the enjoyment of men. That is all foolishness. A tiger may say, "Man was created for me" and pray, "O Lord, how wicked are these men who do not come and place themselves before me to be eaten; they are breaking Your law." If the world is created for us, we are also created for the world. That this world is created for our enjoyment is the most wicked idea that holds us down. This world is not for our sake. Millions pass out of it every year; the world does not feel it; millions of others are supplied in their place. Just as much as the world is for us, so we also are for the world.'

6.2 PRACTICE OF WITNESSHOOD

Another requirement of karma yoga is that we do not mix in the fray, but hold ourselves as the witness and go on working. We must practise the attitude of a nurse engaged in a house. She looks after the children put under her care with all attention, but does not hesitate in the least when she has to leave them and go away. 'Even so are you to be with all that you consider your own. You are the nurse, and if you believe in God, believe that all these things which you consider yours are really His. The greatest weakness often insinuates itself as the greatest good and strength. It is a weakness to think that any one is dependent on me, and that I can do good to another. This belief is the mother of all our attachment, and through this attachment comes all our pain. We must inform our minds that no one in this universe depends upon us; not one beggar depends on our charity; not one soul on our kindness; not one living thing on our help. All are helped on by nature, and will be so helped even though millions of us were not here. The course of nature will not stop for such as you and me; it is, as already pointed out, only a blessed privilege to you and to me that we are allowed, in the way of helping others, to educate ourselves.' The cultivation of this attitude in all our activities in life will generate detachment in us, and help us rise above the good and evil effects of action. The sign of a detached person is that good or ill fortune causes no change in his mind; in all conditions he continues to be the same. 'To those who have not controlled their own minds, the world is either full of evil or at best a mixture of good and evil. This very world will become to us an optimistic world when we become masters of our own minds. Nothing will then work upon us as good or evil; we shall find everything to be in its proper place, to be harmonious. Some men, who begin by saying that the world is a hell, often end by saying that it is a heaven when they succeed in the practice of self-control. If we are genuine Karma-Yogis and wish to train ourselves to that attainment of this state, wherever we may begin we are sure to end in perfect self-abnegation; and as soon as this seeming self has gone, the whole world, which at first appears to us to be filled with evil, will appear to be heaven itself and full of blessedness. Its very atmosphere will be blessed; every human face there will be god. Such is the end and aim of Karma-Yoga, and such is its perfection in practical life.'

6.3 *PRAVRITTI* AND *NIVRITTI*

'Here are two Sanskrit words. The one is Pravritti, which means revolving towards, and the other is Nivritti, which means revolving away. The "revolving towards" is what we call the world, the "I and mine"; it includes all those things which are always enriching that "me" by wealth and money and power, and name and fame, and which are of a grasping nature, always tending to accumulate everything in one centre, that centre being "myself". That is the Pravritti, the natural tendency of every human being; taking everything from everywhere and heaping it around one centre, that centre being man's own sweet self. When this tendency begins to break, when it is Nivritti or "going away from," then begin morality and religion. Both Pravritti and Nivritti are of the nature of work: the former is evil work, and the latter is good work. This Nivritti is the fundamental basis of all morality and all religion, and the very perfection of it is entire self-abnegation, readiness to sacrifice mind and body and everything for another being. When a man has reached that state, he has attained to the perfection of Karma-Yoga. This is the highest result of good works. Although a man has not studied a single system of philosophy, although he does not believe in any God, and never has believed, although he has not prayed even once in his whole life, if the simple power of good actions has brought him to that state where he is ready to give up his life and all else for others, he has arrived at the same point to which the religious man will come through his prayers and the philosopher through his knowledge; and so you may find that the philosopher, the worker, and the devotee, all meet at one point, that one point being self-abnegation. However much their systems of philosophy and religion may differ, all mankind stand in reverence and awe before the man who is ready to sacrifice himself for others.'

'Each one of our Yogas is fitted to make man perfect even without the help of the others, because they have all the same goal in view. The Yogas of work, of wisdom, and of devotion are all capable of serving as direct and independent means for the attainment of Moksha. "Fools alone say that work and philosophy are different, not the learned." The learned know that, though apparently different from each other, they at last lead to the same goal of human perfection.'

7

THE IDEAL OF FREEDOM

The word karma, besides meaning work, also implies the law of moral conservation, the application of the inevitable sequence of cause and effect to the moral realm. By law is meant this tendency of a series to repeat itself. It is more correct to say that this tendency is in our mind rather than in nature; for it is an expectation that this series will repeat itself. 'Certain phenomena, happening one after another or together, and followed by the conviction of the regularity of their recurrence—thus enabling our minds to grasp the method of the whole series—constitute what we call law.'

Law is possible only within this conditioned universe. Our universe is only that portion of existence which is limited by our mind—this universe of the senses which we see, feel, touch, hear, think or imagine. It is only when 'being' or 'existence' gets moulded into name and form that it obeys the law of causation. For this reason, as we understand it, cannot be free; for it is cast in the mould of time, space and causation. But that which gets converted into human will is free.

This universe comes from freedom, rests in bondage, and goes back to freedom. It is only a speck of the Infinite Being, and all our experiences, expectations, progressions and digressions are within that, the sphere of bondage and limitation. Even the heavens that man pictures are only repetitions of his experiences here, though they may be more ethereal than this earth of ours, and enjoyments there, keener than here. To acquire freedom we have to get beyond this limited universe, human and divine, and this is not possible until we give up the thirst after life, our attachment to our own transient condition.

Two ways are laid down for this—one called '*neti, neti*' (not this, not this), and the other '*iti, iti*' (this, this). The first is for men of gigantic will, whose mind and body obey their will, and who can therefore reject the life of bondage and rise into freedom. Such men are very rare. Theirs is the way of *jnana* or reasoning. The second is the path for the vast majority—the way through the world, 'making use of all the bondages themselves to break those very bondages.' This is the path of work. Abandoning of attachment is involved in this also, but 'it is done slowly and gradually, by knowing things, enjoying things and thus obtaining experience ... until the mind lets them all go at last and becomes unattached.'

Each one's individual life is like a quantity of water in a stream that rushes forward, but gets into a hollow, goes round and round for a time as a whirlpool, and then rushes out again towards its destination of freedom forming whirlpools again on the way. The whole universe, including all *jivas* in it, is flying away from bondage, without being aware of it. The trend of life is in that direction, only man does not know it. Karma yoga asks man to be aware of this truth, and try to use the forces of work involved in life to gain this freedom instead of being knocked about in the repetitive process of this world, known as *samsara*.

7.2 NON-ATTACHMENT AS THE WAY TO FREEDOM

Non-attachment is its method. Misery comes through attachment, not work. Attachment is the sense of identification with anything as 'mine'. With the idea of possession comes selfishness, and selfishness brings misery. The more we say 'I' and 'mine', the more slavery grows, and the more misery too. 'Do not even say "my child" in your mind. Possess the child, but do not say "mine". If you do, then will come the misery. Do not say "my house," do not say "my body". The whole difficulty is there. The body is neither yours, nor mine, nor anybody's. These bodies are coming and going by the laws of nature, but we are free, standing as witness. This body is no more free than a picture or a wall. Why should we be attached so much to a body? If somebody paints a picture, he does it and passes on. Do not project that tentacle of selfishness, "I must possess it". As soon as that is projected, misery will begin.'

Not to avoid work or the world, but to be unaffected by it like a lotus leaf in water—is the ideal. This type of non-attached attitude is called *vairagya*, and practice of no yoga is possible without something of it. *vairagya* is essentially in the mind. 'A man may be on a throne and perfectly non-attached; another man may be in rags and still very much attached.' A man may leave all things and go into a forest, but his only possession, the body, can become an obsession for him and make him live a life of intense attachment.

7.3 FAITH IN GOD MAKES NON-ATTACHMENT EASY

There are two ways of practising non-attachment. The first is for those who do not accept a God; for, karma yoga is relevant for them too. Reflecting on the nature of the world, they must discriminate and abandon attachment by the power of their will. But 'For those who believe in God there is another way, which is much less difficult. They give up the fruits of work unto the Lord; they work and are never attached to the results. Whatever they see, feel, hear, or do, is for Him. For whatever

good work we may do, let us not claim any praise or
benefit. It is the Lord's; give up the fruits unto Him.
Let us stand aside and think that we are only servants
obeying the Lord, our Master, and that every impulse
for action comes from Him every moment. Whatever
thou worshippest, whatever thou perceivest, whatever
thou doest, give up all unto Him and be at rest. Let us
be at peace, perfect peace, with ourselves, and give up
our whole body and mind and everything as an eternal
sacrifice unto the Lord. Instead of the sacrifice of pour-
ing oblations into the fire, perform this one great sacrifice day and night—the sacrifice of your little self. "In
search of wealth in this world, Thou art the only wealth
I have found; I sacrifice myself unto Thee. In search of
some one to be loved, Thou art the only one beloved I
have found; I sacrifice myself unto Thee." Let us repeat
this day and night, and say, "Nothing for me; no matter
whether the thing is good, bad, or indifferent; I do not
care for it; I sacrifice all unto Thee!' " This sacrifice of
our seeming self must become a habit with us.

7.4 LIMITATIONS OF THE CONCEPT OF DUTY

Karma yoga expects us to do our duty, but wants us
to rise to a higher plane where we are not the slaves of
duty. Ordinarily the sense of duty degenerates to the
extent of making a man a prisoner of it. Sheer slavery—

morbid attachment of flesh for flesh—is sometimes interpreted as duty. Attachment, 'when it is chronic, we call
it nature. It is a disease. So when attachment becomes
chronic, we baptise it with the high-sounding name of
duty. We strew flowers upon it, trumpets sound for it,
sacred texts are said over it, and then the whole world
fights, and men earnestly rob each other for this duty's
sake. Duty is good to the extent that it checks brutality. To the lowest kinds of men, who cannot have any
other ideal, it is of some good; but those who want to
be Karma-Yogis must throw this idea of duty overboard.
There is no duty for you and me. Whatever you have
to give to the world, do give by all means, but not as
a duty. Do not take any thought of that. Be not compelled. Why should you be compelled? *Everything that
you do under compulsion goes to build up attachment.* Why
should you have any duty? Resign everything unto God.
In this tremendous fiery furnace where the fire of duty
scorches everybody, drink this cup of nectar and be
happy. We are all simply working out His will, and have
nothing to do with rewards and punishments. ... Seek
no praise, on reward, for anything you do. No sooner
do we perform a good action than we begin to desire
credit for it. ... Misery must come as the result of such
desires. The greatest men in the world have passed away
unknown. The Buddhas and the Christs that we know
are but second-rate heroes in comparison with the great-

est men of whom the world knows nothing. ... Silently
they live and silently they pass away; and in time their
thoughts find expression in Buddhas or Christs, and it is
these latter that become known to us. ... These Sattvika
men are too near the Lord to be active and to fight, to
be working, struggling, preaching and doing good, as
they say, here on earth to humanity. The active workers,
however good, have still a little remnant of ignorance
left in them. When our nature has yet some impurities
left in it, then alone can we work. It is in the nature of
work to be impelled ordinarily by motive and by attachment. In the presence of an ever active Providence who
notes even the sparrow's fall, how can man attach any
importance to his own work? Will it not be a blasphemy
to do so when we know that He is taking care of the
minutest things in the world? We have only to stand
in awe and reverence before Him saying, "Thy will be
done". The highest men cannot work, for in them there
is no attachment. Those whose whole soul is gone into
the Self, those whose desires are confined in the Self,
who have become ever associated with the Self, for them
there is no work. Such are indeed the highest of mankind; but apart from them every one else has to work.
In so working we should never think that we can help
on even the least thing in this universe. We cannot. We
only help ourselves in this gymnasium of the world. This
is the proper attitude of work. If we work in this way,

if we always remember that our present opportunity to work thus is a privilege which has been given to us, we shall never be attached to anything. Millions like you and me think that we are great people in the world; but we all die, and in five minutes the world forgets us. But the life of God is infinite. "Who can live a moment, breathe a moment, if this all-powerful One does not will it?" He is the ever active Providence. All power is His and within His command. Through His command the winds blow, the sun shines, the earth lives, and death stalks upon the earth. He is the all in all; He is all and in all. We can only worship Him. Give up all fruits of work; do good for its own sake; then alone will come perfect non-attachment. The bonds of the heart will thus break, and we shall reap perfect freedom. This freedom is indeed the goal of Karma-Yoga.'

7.5 THE IDEAL OF KARMA YOGA

The four yogas, however, are not exclusive of each other. They represent the types of minds in the world; but in practice they often blend, as there are many blends in types of men too. The divisions into yogas are made only on the basis of the dominance of one type of character or another. But all of them have a common goal, and that is freedom. The struggle for freedom is the elemental impulse in the universe. Everything has a tendency to infinite dispersion, to go out of its limited individuality and dissolve into the freedom of the boundless. The reflection of this tendency in the ethical realm is morality. In unselfishness, the basis of all morality, this tendency is witnessed. Absolute unselfishness means infinite expansion. Even a personalist who accepts morality can be brought under this description. For he has to be one with the whole universe to become perfectly selfless. The personalist is, however, reluctant to accept a corresponding reasoning or metaphysics.

'Karma-Yoga, therefore, is a system of ethics and religion intended to attain freedom through unselfishness, and by good works. The Karma-Yogi need not believe in any doctrine whatever. He may not believe even in God, may not ask what his soul is, nor think of any metaphysical speculation. He has got his own special aim of realising selflessness; and he has to work it out himself. Every moment of his life must be realisation, because he has to solve by mere work, without the help of doctrine or theory, the very same problem to which the Jnāni applies his reason and inspiration and the Bhakta his love.'

7.6 LIMITATIONS OF ALTRUISM

The work of a karma yogin must, however, be based on a proper outlook on the world in which he has to live. It must be based on a proper understanding of its nature. Otherwise work, even when sincere, will lead him only to fanaticism.

What is the nature of the world? It is imperfect and full of inequalities. There is an urge in man to set right these imperfections and inequalities, but a philosophic outlook will tell him that, while this aim may be partially achieved in patches or segments of the world, it is impossible in the fullest sense. 'Can any permanent happiness be given to the world? ... The sum total of the good things in the world has been the same throughout in its relation to man's need and greed. It cannot be increased or decreased. Take the history of the human race as we know it today. Do we not find the same miseries and the same happiness, the same pleasures and pains, the same differences in position? Are not some rich, some poor, some high, some low, some healthy, some unhealthy? All this was just the same with the Egyptians, the Greeks, and the Romans in ancient times as it is with the Americans today. So far as history is known, it has always been the same; yet at the same time we find that, running along with all these incurable differences of pleasure and pain, there has ever been the struggle to alleviate them. Every period of history has given birth to thousands of men and women who have worked hard to smooth the passage of life for others. And how far have they succeeded? We can only play at driving the ball from one place to another. We take away the pain from the physical plane, and it goes to the mental one. ... All our talks about the millennium are very nice as school-boy's stories, but they are no better than that. All nations that dream of the millennium also think that, of all peoples in the world, they will have the best of it then for themselves.'

'In modern times the millennium aspiration takes the form of equality—of liberty, equality, and fraternity. This is also fanaticism. True equality has never been and never can be on earth. ... What makes the difference between man and man? It is largely the difference in the brain. ... We come into the world with unequal endowments; we come as greater men or as lesser men, and there is no getting away from that pre-natally determined condition. ... Perfect equality will come only when a cycle of creation comes to its end.'

'Yet this idea of realising the millennium is a great motive power. Just as inequality is necessary for creation itself, so the struggle to limit it is also necessary. If there were no struggle to become free and get back to God, there would be no creation either. It is the difference between these two forces that determines the nature of the motives of men. There will always be these motives to work, some tending towards bondage and others towards freedom.'

7.7 THE IDEAL OF WORKING WITHOUT FANATICISM

A karma yogin must understand this nature of the world and be free from fanaticism as the motive power of his activity. Even while knowing that the imperfections of the world will continue, he must have the urge to do good as an innate tendency. This is realised to the extent that a person has become unselfish. '*That which is selfish is immoral, and that which is unselfish is moral.*'—this must be the motto of a true karma yogin. Instead of external motives to stimulate him to action, the inner urge of love and goodness must take its place. Then only freedom from attachment and fanaticism can be realised.

The one striking example of a man given to good action without any external motive was the Buddha. Without any theory of a God, he exhorted man to do good for its own sake. 'This great philosopher, preaching the highest philosophy, yet had the deepest sympathy for the lowest of animals, and never put forth any claims for himself. He is the ideal Karma-Yogi, acting entirely without motive, and the history of humanity shows him to have been the greatest man ever born; beyond compare the greatest combination of heart and brain that ever existed, the greatest soul-power that has even been manifested.'

8

RESUME—THE GIST OF SWAMI VIVEKANANDA'S KARMA YOGA

Karma yoga is the way by means of which man's will power as expressed in action is utilised for his spiritual development. All powers and excellences are given in the human spirit; and thoughts and actions are the means by which they are elicited and expressed in terms of character or personality. Actions are like waves in the ocean. However small, they do not perish, but combine together to produce a huge wave. So are actions of men, and the Buddhas and the Christs of the world are the end-products—huge waves—of a long series of actions done from a right motivation.

Generally all actions of men are selfishly motivated. Selfish action done for immediate results do not elicit the higher spiritual power of man. The moral energies are dissipated by such actions and only a spiritual stalemate, or even degradation, is the result. The moral energies are conserved only when actions are prompted by pure love, without any motivation of selfishness, and done with detachment. To attain to these excellences and thereby complete the spiritual evolution of man, is the ideal of karma yoga.

But this highest ideal is not achieved all at once. Man has to go through the school of duty before he is fit for this higher development. Duty varies from man to man, from one state in life to another, from time to time, and from community to community. To present the highest ideal alone and condemn all who cannot come up to that, is an unhealthy habit. It creates inferiority complex and self-condemnation in man. This is very detrimental to man's progress. The Indian tradition therefore maintains that every order of life, whether of the householder or the *sannyasin*, is equally good, if the duties appertaining to it are properly performed. Proper performance of duty without selfish attachment leads to spiritual progress. Reference has been made to the story of the dutiful woman, the *sannyasin* and the butcher.

But care must be taken to see that duty does not degenerate into hypocrisy, prompting men to self-aggrandizement, exploitation and selfish attachments under the guise of duty. So also duty should not become a prison house or a cause of enslavement for man. The more one has a sense of resignation to a higher will and one eliminates pure selfishness from one's motivation, the more will one become successful in this.

While love of God and resignation of all the fruits of

one's action to Him and cultivation of a sense of being
only His instrument are helpful in the practice of karma
yoga, even persons who have no such belief can become
ideal karma yogins if they are motivated by pure love
and goodness, if they are unattached in action, and seek
no personal rewards for themselves. This becomes possible only under the three following conditions: (1) By
repeatedly doing good action, a man must reach a state
when he has become incapable of doing harm to others;
(2) He must be free from petty desires and ambitions;
(3) He must have a philosophic outlook.

Like all other yogas, karma yoga also has got freedom as its ideal. To be free from all selfishness is freedom, and if one is absolutely free from the hold of the
narrow little self and is full of love and detachment, he
reaches the same goal of spiritual freedom as those who
pursue the other yogas.

A conspicuous example of perfection through good
action is that of the Buddha.

PART 2: RAJA YOGA

9

PROLOGUE

9.1 CAN RELIGION BE MADE SCIENTIFIC?

All real knowledge is based upon experience. Science formulates its laws by bringing together all the experiences of the particulars under certain generalisations. These generalisations are formulated through reasoning based on the particulars observed. So when scientific laws are propounded, people find their truth easily, because they appeal to the experiences of every human being.

Is anything like this possible in regard to religion? Generally religion is supposed to ask people to believe, i.e. accept propositions without calling for proofs of their truths, and we therefore find that religions are generally based on doctrines accepted on the basis of scriptural authority. 'Nevertheless, there is a basis of universal belief in religion, governing all the different theories and all the varying ideas of different sects in different countries. Going to their basis we find that they also are based upon universal experiences. ... The teachers all saw God; they all saw their own souls, they saw their future, they saw their eternity, and what they saw they preached. Only there is this difference that by most of these religions especially in modern times, a peculiar claim is made, namely, that these experiences are impossible at the present day; they were only possible with a few men, who were the first founders of the religions that subsequently bore their names. At the present time these experiences have become obsolete, and, therefore, we have now to take religion on belief. This I entirely deny. If there has been one experience in this world in any particular branch of knowledge, it absolutely follows that that experience has been possible millions of times before, and will be repeated eternally. Uniformity is the rigorous law of nature; what once happened can happen always. The teachers of the science of Yoga, therefore, declare that religion is not only based upon the experience of ancient times, but that no man can be religious until he has the same perceptions himself. Yoga is the science which teaches us how to get these perceptions.'

9.2 THE CLAIMS OF YOGA TO MAKE RELIGION SCIENTIFIC

The system of raja yoga proposes to place before humanity a scientifically worked out technique for the attainment of these higher spiritual perceptions about the nature of man and the universe. Each science has got its own method, and without trying that in all earnestness and sincerity, we shall not be rational in denying the truth of their assertion. In the case of the sciences of the external world, the problem is to train the mind to observe external facts in a systematic way. But the knowledge of our own mind, that is, of the internal nature of man, can never be had until we have mastered the technique of observing the facts that are going on within. And the science of raja yoga offers us this means for training ourselves in the observation of internal states.

'The instrument is the mind itself. The power of attention, when properly guided, and directed towards the internal world, will analyse the mind, and illumine facts for us. The powers of the mind are like the rays dissipated; when they are concentrated, they illumine. This is the only means of knowledge. ... From our childhood upwards we have been taught only to pay attention to things external, but never to things internal; hence most of us have nearly lost the faculty of observing the internal mechanism. To turn the mind, as it were, inside, stop it from going outside, and then to concentrate all its powers, and throw them upon the mind itself, in order that it may know its own nature, analyse itself, is very hard work. Yet that is the only way to anything which will be a scientific approach to the subject.'

9.3 THE NATURE OF CONCENTRATION

All knowledge has been gained only by the power of concentration. When it is applied to external objects, the natural sciences develop, and when applied to the internal world, we get raja yoga, the science of religion. All persons have, in a small degree, this power of reflection—of standing aside by a part of the mind and with that observing the various movements of the mind and actions resulting from them. This capacity of the mind to be its own witness or observer has to be developed.

The mind is an instrument in the hands of the soul, and it is constantly vacillating from one subject to another. In our ordinary state when the mind is attached intently to one organ, say, that of hearing while listening to music, it may not perceive through the other organs like the eyes, though they may be open. 'But the perfected mind can be attached to all the organs simultaneously. It has the reflexive power of looking back into its own depths. This reflexive power is what the Yogi wants to attain; by concentrating the powers of the mind, and turning them inward, he seeks to know what is happening inside. There is in this no question of mere belief; it is the analysis arrived at by certain philosophers. Modern physiologists tell us that the eyes are not the organ of vision, but that the organ is in one of the nerve centres of the brain, and so with all the senses; they also tell us that these centres are formed of the same material as the brain itself. The Sankhyas also tell us the same thing. The former is a statement on the physical side, and the latter on the psychological side; yet both are the same. Our field of research lies beyond this.

The Yogi proposes to attain that fine state of perception in which he can perceive all the different mental states. There must be mental perception of all of them. One can perceive how the sensation is travelling, how the mind is receiving it, how it is going to the determinative faculty, and how this gives it to the Purusha.'

The question of faith in any particular cult or adherence to any particular religion is inconsequential in raja yoga. All men are eligible provided they have the requisite earnestness and moral fitness. What these are will be discussed in later sections.

10

LIMBS OF YOGA

Raja yoga is divided into eight steps. These are (1) *yama*, which consists in the practice of non-injury, truthfulness, non-stealing, continence, and non-reception of gifts; (2) *niyama* consisting in cleanliness, contentment, austerity, study and self-surrender to God; (3) asana or bodily posture; (4) pranayama or control of vital energy; (5) *pratyahara* or restraint of the senses from their objects; (6) *dharana* or fixing of the mind on a spot; (7) *dhyana* or meditation; and (8) samadhi or superconsciousness.

The first two steps, it will be seen, are moral disciplines. Unless an aspirant has attained success in the practice of these disciplines, the practice of the subsequent steps of yoga will be ineffective. Those who practise yogas, very often forget this, and are taken up with various forms of physical postures called asanas and pranayama. While these may have considerable value as physical exercises, they have no spiritual impact unless they are backed up by a strong moral and spiritual aspiration.

10.2 THE PROPER PLACE OF ASANA IN YOGA

The third step asana is important in raja yoga only in so far as one must have practice to sit for long periods in a firm posture that is conducive to meditation. The essence of it is that the spine should be held relaxed and erect, with the three upper parts of the body, the chest, the neck and the head, held in a straight line, and the weight of the upper part of the body evenly distributed on the ribs. In the practice of concentration nerve currents will have to go through new channels, and the main part of this activity of a very subtle nature will lie along the spinal column. Hence the importance of holding the spine erect.

The practice of asanas is elaborated in hatha yoga which is mainly concerned with the maintenance of the health and attainment of the longevity of the body. While some of these postures will be helpful in the maintenance of health, they always present a pitfall to man. For, getting too much engrossed in them will make man only body- minded, while the object of yoga is to make man rise above body-consciousness. The true yogi should never forget that the body is his, and not he the body's. Health and bodily care are needed because an unhealthy body always stands in the way of practising meditation; for disease is an obstacle to yoga. Similarly doubt in the science of yoga is also an obstacle which may be removed considerably by experiences derived from yoga.

10.3 PURIFICATION OF THE NERVES

After a firm and erect sitting posture is mastered, what is called the purification of the nerves has to be practised as a preliminary step according to some. This practice is thus described: 'Stopping the right nostril with the thumb, through the left nostril fill in air, according to capacity; then, without any interval, throw the air out through the right nostril, closing the left one. Again inhaling through the right nostril eject through the left, according to capacity; practicing this three or five times at four hours of the day, before dawn, during midday, in the evening, and at midnight, in fifteen days or a month purity of the nerves is attained; then begins Pranayama.'

10.4 THE RATIONALE OF PRANAYAMA

Pranayama is generally described as breath control. What breath has to do with the practice of concentration, the subject with which raja yoga is concerned, requires an explanation. Breath is like the flywheel of the machine, the body. In a big engine you find the flywheel first moving, and the motion is conveyed to finer and finer machinery until the finest and the most delicate mechanism in the machine is in motion. The breath is that flywheel, regulating and supplying the motive power to everything in this body. We know very little of our bodies and minds, of the fine process within, that keep bright the lamp of life and thought. The reason for this is that only when the mind becomes very subtle, can it enter into the depth of our being and watch the subtle movements of the body. 'To get the subtle perception we have to begin with the grosser perceptions. We have to get hold of that which is setting the whole engine in motion. That is the Prana, the most obvious manifestation of which is the breath. Then, along with the breath, we shall slowly enter the body, which will enable us to find out about the subtle forces, the nerve currents that are moving all through the body. As soon as we perceive and learn to feel them, we shall begin to get control over them, and over the body. The mind also is set in motion by these different nerve currents, so at last we shall reach the state of perfect control over the body and the mind, making both our servants. Knowledge is power. We have to get this power. So we must begin at the beginning, with Pranayama, restraining the Prana.'

For those who take to these practices seriously, it is better to have a room reserved for these purposes, so that it may be full of holy vibrations. Seating oneself in a convenient posture, one must first send out good thoughts for the welfare of all beings everywhere. Then one must salute and pray to God for knowledge and light.

11

PRANA

Pranayama does not really mean control of breath, but the control of the universal energy, prana, that moves the whole universe. Indian thinkers analyse the whole of the manifested universe into two ultimate entities—akasha and prana. Akasa is the ultimate or basic stuff out of which all the gross forms, from galaxies to atoms, from microscopic cells to the perfected human and divine bodies, take shape, and into which they resolve when they are dissolved or disintegrated to the pristine condition. Akasa, the matrix of all forms, cannot itself be perceived. It is experienced only as its gross effects or combinations.

What works upon the akasha and shapes it into all forms or manifestations is called prana, the name for that all-inclusive basic energy into which all forms of energy known to us as manifesting in matter and mind are reduced at the end of the cycle. It is prana vibrating at the beginning of the cosmic cycle that shapes akasa, the basic condition of matter, into a new universe of diverse forms and states of subtlety. Out of prana is evolved also all forms of energy, physical or mental. Thus all physical forces like motion, electricity, magnetism and the rest are expressions of prana. All the biological functions in the body, the functions of the nerve currents and the operation of the mind are also aspects of prana. Thus the sum total of all forces in the universe, mental and physical, when resolved back to their original state, is prana. The knowledge and control of this prana is the real meaning of pranayama.

Now the quantum of prana working our mind and body is the nearest to us of all the waves of the infinite ocean of prana. The yogi who has been able to establish control over the quantum of prana constituting his being, is able to establish a kind of mastery over prana as such; for, as the whole universe is one mass of prana and akasha, one who has established control over it in oneself, is able to be in touch with the whole.

11.2 PRANA AND THE MIND

Thought is the highest expression of prana. Its expression is threefold. First there is instinct, which may be called unconscious thought. At a higher level is reason in which thought is a conscious and well-regulated effort. But the circle within which it runs is very limited. That which is beyond it is grasped by super-consciousness or samadhi. All manipulations of the subtle forces of the body, which are different manifestations of prana, give a push to the mind to assume vibrations which reveal facts at subtle levels of existence. The whole universe is one unbroken mass of matter in flux beaten into different states of vibration by the prana. Of this one huge mass, one point is called a moon, another a sun, another a man, another a plant, another a mineral and so on. When the action of prana on akasha is most subtle, it is called mind. Mind is also one unbroken continuum. If one gets into that subtle vibration through the regulation of prana within oneself, then the whole universe is seen as composed of subtle vibrations of thought. Samadhi brings the individual's mind to those vibrations which enable it to apprehend the facts of these subtle levels of existence.

11.3 CONNECTION BETWEEN PRANA AND BREATH

Pranayama is the discipline for establishing control over prana in oneself and for bringing it into vibrations that are helpful in attaining to higher insight and understanding. The most obvious movement of the prana in the body is the motion of the lungs in breathing. In breathing, it is not that breath is producing the motion

of the lungs. It is the motion of the lungs that helps
the air to be drawn in by pump action. Pranayama is
nothing but controlling that muscular power which
moves the lungs. That power which goes out through
the nerves to the lungs, moving them in a certain manner, is the prana, and it is this that one learns to control
through pranayama. When this expression of prana
through breathing is controlled by an aspirant, all other
actions of the prana in the body will slowly come under
his control.

11.4 PRANA AND COSMIC VIBRATION

It is by the power of controlled prana that faith healing is effected. The man who has controlled the prana
has the power of bringing it into a certain state of vibration which can be conveyed to others, arousing in
them a similar vibration. It is in this way that faith
cure is effected. It is also the secret of the power of
great men over others. 'The gigantic will-powers of the
world, the world-movers, can bring their Prana into a
high state of vibration, and it is so great and powerful
that it catches others in a moment, and thousands are
drawn towards them, and half the world think as they
do. Great prophets of the world had the most wonderful control of the Prana, which gave them tremendous
will-power; they had brought their Prana to the highest

state of motion, and this is what gave them power to sway the world. All manifestations of power arise from this control.' In spirituality also the manipulation of the power of prana is evident. The universe perceived by our senses is the manifestation of akasha by the vibration of prana at a certain state of intensity. All of us too are in a certain state of vibration and we are aware of others like us in the same state of vibration. But there are innumerable other universes, representing the vibrations of prana in akasha at different intensities, simultaneously existing, inter-crossing, as it were without obtruding into one another in any way, because of the difference in the degrees of the vibrations they represent. Each vibration in akasha is a sphere with its own denizens, having their lives, oblivious of all others. Now if a yogi can change the vibrations of his mind and attune himself to any of these vibrations representing any of the spheres, he can become aware of those spheres while simultaneously becoming shut off from his earthly contacts. All these kinds of supra- conscious experiences come under samadhi. The lowest rungs of supra-conscious experiences come under spiritism. But the highest grade samadhi is when we realise that unitary substance out of which all these vibrations and beings representing them have come.

11.5 YOGA AS A MEANS FOR EXPEDITING EVOLUTION

Now the whole panorama of life reveals a natural urge to develop from lower states of consciousness to higher. Starting as some fungus, some very minute microscopic bubble, and all the time drawing from that infinite storehouse of energy, the form of the fungus is changed slowly and steadily until in course of time it becomes a plant, then an animal, then man, and ultimately God. This is attained through millions of aeons of time. But the progress can be expedited at the human level. The idea of the yogi, the whole science of yoga, is to shorten this time of gaining perfection with the help of disciplines that go to intensify man's power of perception. Pranayama is one of the important parts of this discipline according to raja yoga. The methods by which physical manifestation of prana like light, electricity, magnetism etc., are controlled is called applied science; and the methods adopted for controlling the manifestation of prana as vital and mental force, through psychical means, is called raja yoga.

12

THE PSYCHIC PRANA

12.1 THE PLACE OF PRANAYAMA IN ROUSING THE KUNDALINI

The term psychic prana includes in a broad sense all the vital energy working in the nervous and other systems of the body, and particularly the latent or coiled up energy at the base of the spinal column, technically called kundalini or 'coiled up' power. The object of pranayama is to control the functioning of the vital energy in the body, through the control established over the breath, and utilise the power so generated to rouse the kundalini.

It has already been said that breathing is like the flywheel of a machine. By regulating its movement, the movements of the finer and the very finest of the cogs working in the machine can be regulated. The control of the breathing process works similarly on all the functioning of the prana in the body. By rhythmic breathing all the molecules of the body gradually begin to move in the same direction and this makes man a tremendous battery of will-power. It is analogous to electricity. When all the electrons in a body flow in the same direction, electric power is generated. So also by the control and direction of all the energies of the body and mind, the yogi becomes a great centre of will-power, which he can utilise to rouse the kundalini.

12.2 THE CONCEPT OF KUNDALINI

The concept of kundalini has to be understood in the context of the yogic conception of the nerve currents in the human body. Modern anatomy teaches that the vertebral column has the spinal cord running through it, starting from the brain and ending in the lumbar vertebrae as fine nerve fibres. On the two sides of the spinal cord are the two nerve currents, *ida* and *pingala*, corresponding to the anatomist's afferent nerve which carries sensations to the brain, and the efferent nerve which conveys the reaction of the brain to the body. Now between these two currents is what the yogi calls *sushumna*, a canal identified with, or considered corresponding to, *canal centralis*. It is a canal closed at the bottom and is functionless in man ordinarily.

Now the effort of the yogi is to open up this canal and let the nerve current, usually traversing only along the *ida* and the *pingala*, pass through this hollow canal without the help of any transmission wire like the nerves. The nervous system, evolved by nature in the course of evolution as the medium of contact for consciousness with the environment, has practically become the prison-house of consciousness and fixed it in identification with the body. To break this bondage of the body, the yogi opens the *sushumna* and sends the mental currents through its empty space without any nerve fibre to act as wire.

At the lowest level of the spinal column is the sacral plexus or the *muladhara* (root receptacle), which is also the seat of the kundalini, the 'coiled up' power of evolutionary impulse, which after producing the body, sleeps as it were at this plexus. It is roused up by the tremendous concentrated will-power generated by pranayama. All the 'residual motor energy' and 'residual sensations' are stored up in the *muladhara* and are included in the concept of kundalini.

A faint working of the kundalini is noticed in the dream phenomena. In the dream we have vivid perceptions. Perceptions generally take place when the concerned nerves are stimulated from outside; so there must also be an internal source to give such stimulation in the case of dreams. It comes from the kundalini, where all the energy of latent impressions is stored up. The manifestation of a little of it generates the creativeness and sense of reality one gets in the experience of dreams and vivid imagination.

12.3 WHAT HAPPENS WHEN
THE KUNDALINI IS ROUSED

Now the yogi proposes to rouse this latent power in
its entirety. It is with the tremendous will-power generated through pranayama that the kundalini is roused
up and made to open the *sushumna* canal and go up to
the brain centre. In the course of its ascent it touches
and enlivens the six plexes called chakras. The enliv-
ening of each of these chakras reveals subtler and subtler planes of consciousness to the yogi along with the
experiences that pertain to each. All our experiences
are had in some kind of space. We have our ordinary
sense experiences in the *mahakasa*, the elemental space.
The subtler perceptions and the psychic powers that
the rousing of the kundalini brings, are experienced
in *chittakasa* or mental space. When the kundalini has
reached the end of the canal which opens out into the
brain, consciousness becomes objectless experience, and
the soul shines in its own nature without the bondage
of the body, gross or subtle. This objectless perception
is called *chidakasa* or knowledge-sphere.

'Now, if this coiled-up energy be roused and made
active, and then consciously made to travel up the Sushumna canal, as it acts upon centre after centre, a tremendous reaction will set in. When a minute portion
of energy travels along a nerve fibre and causes reac-

tion from centres, the perception is either dream or imagination. But when by the power of long internal meditation the vast mass of energy stored up travels along the Sushumna, and strikes the centres, the reaction is tremendous, immensely superior to the reaction of dream or imagination, immensely more intense than the reaction of sense-perception. It is super-sensuous perception. And when it reaches the metropolis of all sensations, the brain, the whole brain, as it were, reacts, and the result is the full blaze of illumination, the perception of the Self. As this Kundalini force travels from centre to centre, layer after layer of the mind, as it were, opens up, and this universe is perceived by the Yogi in its fine, or causal form. Then alone the causes of this universe, both as sensation and reaction, are known as they are, and hence comes all knowledge. The causes being known, the knowledge of the effects is sure to follow.

Thus the rousing of the Kundalini is the one and only way to attaining Divine Wisdom, superconscious perception, realisation of the spirit. The rousing may come in various ways, through love for God, through the mercy of perfected sages, or through the power of the analytic will of the philosopher. Wherever there was any manifestation of what is ordinarily called supernatural power or wisdom, there a little current of Kundalini must have found its way into the Sushumna.'

13

THE PSYCHIC PRANA AND ITS CONTROL

13.1 EXERCISES IN PRANAYAMA

Pranayama, as it has already been said, is not a kind of breathing exercise, but a means for establishing control over the nerves and muscles involved in breathing, and through that control, over all the finer movements of the prana in the body. Its ultimate purpose is the rousing of the kundalini.

There are three exercises in pranayama, but it is very essential, that before one starts on it, one has learnt to sit steadily erect, with body, neck and head in one line. Sitting crookedly while practising meditation is very injurious, as the spinal cord is adversely affected thereby.

The three exercises in pranayama are as follows:

(1) Breath in and out in a measured way, mentally uttering Om in the process. Breath may be comfortably deep, but is not to be held in. One should breath with awareness, i.e., consciously, unlike what we normally do. By doing this a few times, the body will become restful and rhythmic.

(2) After this practice for some days, the second exercise may be started. Slowly take in the breath through the left nostril, imagining that you are drawing in energy through the *ida* and sending the nerve current down the spinal column and striking forcibly on the *muladhara*, the seat of kundalini. Holding the current there for a while, then breath out slowly through the right nostril, i.e., bring out the current through the *pingala*. Next do it in the reverse manner, i.e., inhale through the right (*pingala*) and exhale through the left (*ida*). The process can be helped by closing and opening the nostrils with the thumb and the forefinger for regulating the breath. The time recommended is four seconds for drawing in, sixteen seconds for retention, and eight seconds for exhalation. The breathing must be accompanied with concentration on the *muladhara* for the rousing of the kundalini.

(3) In the third kind of pranayama, air is inhaled and exhaled as above according to the same time schedule, but air is not retained in. On the other hand, it is exhaled immediately and the breath is held out for the same length of lime as it is held within in the second type of pranayama.

Pranayama should he undertaken only by people who have the physical and moral fitness to practise it. The first exercise described above is a very general exercise and is free from danger. The second one with

retention is especially risky for people who are not fit
for it. To start with, pranayama is to be done only four
times, both morning and evening, but may be care-
fully and cautiously increased by persons who have the
required fitness. While even a little practice will give
more calmness to the body and mind, it is only for those
who can intensify the practice, that the arousing of the
kundalini will be possible.

The kundalini that is awakened rises along the *sushumna* to the brain, in the course of which it touches
the six chakras or centres expanding and deepening the
consciousness. The lowest of the chakras is the *muladhara*, the next higher *swadhishthana*, the third *manipura*,
the fourth *anahata*, the fifth *visuddha*, the sixth *ajna*,
and the last, which is the brain, is called the *sahasrara*
or the thousand-petalled lotus.

13.2 THE CONCEPT OF *OJAS*

It is absolutely necessary that one who seeks to rouse
the kundalini should practise perfect purity and ab-
stinence in sex life. The controlled and sublimated sex
energy becomes *ojas*. *Ojas* is the spiritual vitality that
makes the nervous system and the brain capable of
standing the strains of meditative life. The *ojas* that is
generated by the control and sublimation of sex energy
is stored up in the brain, and the vitality, impressive-

ness and the power of personality in a man are largely dependent on how far his brain is enriched by *ojas*. For a person leading an uncontrolled sex life, practice of raja yoga is very dangerous. It may lead to nervous trouble and even to insanity.

14

PRATYAHARA AND DHARANA

Perceptions take place when the external instruments
of perception convey impressions to the internal organ
in the brain and the mind reacts to the message. Thus
the simultaneous conjunction of the external instrument, the internal organ and the mind are required
to have perceptions. Now withholding the mind from
going along the channels of perception and in gathering it, is *pratyahara*, which literally means 'gathering
towards'.

The capacity to do this is the essence of all self-mas-
tery. Moral instruction consisting in forbidding the
doing of certain things is ineffective, because the power
to detach the mind from the object of the senses is not
present in the person instructed. In hypnosis, a subject
is made to detach his mind from all other sensations by
the technique adopted by the operator, and the subject
becomes capable of taking up the suggestion given by
the operator without any inhibitions. But this has got

possibilities of adverse effect on the subject. For, he becomes subordinate to the will of another, as he is stunned as it were by the operator's will. Long exposure to such influences will devitalise a person's mind. Only control over the mind established by one's own mind is healthy.

Establishing control over the mind is not an easy task. For, the mind is restless like a maddened monkey that has drunk wine and has also been stung by a scorpion. So the first lesson in controlling it is to sit quietly and let the mind run on its own way. It will be jumping about from thought to thought. In place of checking it by force, or being carried away by it, one should keep on watching it. If this is done persistently, it will be observed that the mind's vagaries will gradually decrease and it will learn to stay in a detached state. The more one has got this capacity, the more is one established in *pratyahara*, which is the basis of all further developments in yoga.

14.2 WHAT IS *DHARANA*?

After some practice of *pratyahara*, one should go to the next step, that is, *dharana*, which means holding the mind at a certain point. One may start with holding the mind fixed to an exclusively external object; for external concentration is comparatively easy. Or, one may try to feel only one spot or part of the body, say, the hand, to the exclusion of the rest of the body. Or, one may try to fix the mind in the centre of one's being, which is called ordinarily the heart. To facilitate the *dharana* or fixing of the mind, the help of imagination can also be sought. One may imagine a lotus flower or a flame in the centre of one's being and fix the mind exclusively on it. Fixing of the mind may be done on the various centres of the *sushumna*. Devotees also practise fixing the mind on the form of the Deity they adore.

Long and arduous practice is required for success in *dharana* or complete fixing of the mind. Persons who are very serious in practice should live alone, not talk or work much, and eat sparingly, preferably living on milk and cereals. The early results of successful practice are toning down of nervous excitement, calmness, better temperament, and clearer voice. 'Those who practise hard will get many other signs. Sometimes there will be sounds, as a peal of bells heard at a distance, commingling, and falling on the ear as one continuous sound. Sometimes things will be seen, little specks of light floating and becoming bigger and bigger; and when these things come, know that you are progressing fast. ... When one begins to concentrate, the dropping of a pin will seem like a thunderbolt going through the brain. As the organs get finer, the perceptions get finer. ... Give up all argumentation and other distractions.

... Things of subtler planes have to be realised. Will talking do that? ... Read only those books which have been written by persons who have had realisation.' Be like the pearl oyster, which takes up one drop of water at the right time, goes down to the depths of the water giving up other concerns, and patiently develops the rain drop into a pearl. Thus in place of nibbling at all sorts of things that come in one's way, a genuine aspirant takes up one idea, and makes it his main concern in life. Success attends only on those who have energy, perseverance and moral fitness.

15

DHYANA AND SAMADHI

15.1 WHAT IS SAMADHI? IT'S TEST

In the constitution of man's body and mind, there are some strata of which we are conscious and over which we have got some sort of control, and other strata of which we are not aware and over which we have no control. Thus in our body there are our external limbs and other organs over which we have control. But we have within, our digestive system, circulatory system, etc., over which we have no control and very little awareness. In spite of this fact, even these unconscious activities are done by ourselves and not by any outside agency. It is therefore claimed by yogis that even these can be brought under the conscious control of man.

The point to note is that there are two planes of consciousness—the one which is accompanied by the feeling of egoism and self-consciousness, and the other the unconscious sphere where life is functioning without an ego sense. This demarcation holds good with regard to mental activities also. There is the sphere of our rational mind, wherein self-consciousness accompanied by an individualised will is functioning. There is in contrast the instinctive life, especially in animals, where the mind and body function automatically and without a conscious effort of the will. Thus there are ordinarily two levels of the mind, the Self-consciousness and ego-prompted rational level, and the ego-less and uncontrolled instinctive level.

But the yogis hold that 'the mind goes beyond this line of self-consciousness.' Just as unconscious work is beneath consciousness, so there is another kind of work which is above consciousness and which also is not accompanied with the feeling of egoism. The feeling of egoism is only on the middle plane. When the mind is above or below that line, there is no feeling of 'I', and yet the mind works. When the mind goes beyond this line of self-consciousness, it is called samadhi or super-consciousness. How, for instance, do we know that the man in samadhi has not gone below consciousness, has not degenerated instead of going higher. For, in both cases egoism is not functioning. The answer is, by the effects; by the results of the work we know what is below and what is above. When a man goes into deep sleep, he enters a plane beneath consciousness. But his body works all the time he sleeps, he breathes, he moves the body, perhaps, without any accompanying feeling of ego. He is unconscious, and when he returns from his

sleep, he is the same man who went into it. The sum-
total of the knowledge which he had before he went
into sleep remains the same; it does not increase at all.
No enlightenment has come. But when a man goes into
samadhi, if he goes into it a fool, he comes out a sage a
prophet, a saint, his whole character changed, his life
changed, illumined.

These are the effects. Now the effects being different,
the causes must be different. As this illumination with
which a man comes back from samadhi is much higher
than can be got from unconsciousness, or much higher
than can be got by reasoning in a conscious state, it
must therefore be super-consciousness, and samadhi is
called that superconscious state.

15.2 SAMADHI.THE ONLY PROOF OF RELIGION AND ETHICS

Thus it will be seen that the field of the functioning
of reason is very limited. It moves within a small circle,
and cannot go beyond it. But it is from beyond it that
all that humanity holds most noble, elevating and true
have come. The answer for such questions as whether
there is an immortal soul, whether there is God, a supreme intelligence guiding the destinies of the universe,
is beyond that circle where reason functions. All that
reason can aver on such fundamental questions is that it

cannot say either yes or no. It can only remain agnostic. But without some positive and credible answer to these questions, human life will be purposeless. For, all our ethical theories, our moral attitudes, all that is good and great in human nature have been moulded upon answers that have come from beyond the circle. So it is important that we should have an answer to these questions, and it can come only from the super-conscious state beyond reason.

There are some who find a sanction for ethics in utilitarianism—in the idea that the ethical norm is dictated by the greatest good of the greatest number. But utilitarianism cannot give a rational answer to the question why I should not cause the greatest unhappiness of the greatest number, if that serves my purpose and gives me intense happiness, say, as Nero fiddled enjoying the sight of Rome burning. From the point of view of knowledge gained by the senses and by reasonings based on it, we find no reasons for accepting the good of the largest number as the sanction for action, if the contrary will give us happiness in any measure. The life of the senses and the instinctive level in us, prompt us only to selfishness, and reason cannot convince us why we should not be so. So ethics, for which reason finds no justification, has to seek its foundations in the super-conscious—in that which is beyond the instinctive and the rational self in us. All religions therefore base

their ethics on inspiration, often meaning that they are
dictated by a being beyond our sphere of consciousness.
But the yoga comes and tells us that these prophets
and preachers are correct in telling that it comes from
beyond the circle of reason, but not in concluding that
it comes from somewhere beyond ourselves. For the
yoga maintains that the mind itself has a higher state
of existence beyond reason, a superconscious state, and
when the mind gets to that higher state, truths that are
beyond reasoning come to man. While there have been
cases of men who had attained to this state sporadic-
ally, yoga enables man to that level systematically, and
consequently without any adverse side effects. Sporadic
attainment of samadhi results often in superstitious interpretations of it and in the development of fanatical
attitudes.

15.3 ANALYSIS OF THE PROCESS OF SAMADHI

In order to gain the super-conscious state in a scientific manner, it is necessary to pass through the various stages of concentration—pratyahara, dharana and
samadhi. 'After Pratyāhāra and Dhāranā, we come to
Dhyāna, meditation. When the mind has been trained
to remain fixed on a certain internal or external loca-
tion, there comes to it the power of flowing in an unbroken current, as it were, towards that point. This

state is called Dhyana. When one has so intensified the power of Dhyana as to be able to reject the external part of perception and remain meditating only on the internal part, the meaning, that state is called Samadhi. The three—Dharana, Dhyana, and Samadhi—together, are called Samyama. That is, if the mind can first concentrate upon an object, and then is able to continue in that concentration for a length of time, and then, by continued concentration, to dwell only on the internal part of the perception of which the object was the effect, everything comes under the control of such a mind.'

This meditation must begin with gross objects and slowly rise to finer and finer ones until it becomes objectless. The mind should first be employed in perceiving the external causes of sensations, then the internal motions and then its own reactions. When it has succeeded in perceiving the motions inside by themselves, it will gain the control of all the mental waves in itself or in others, even before they have translated themselves into physical energy; and when he will be able to perceive the mental reaction by itself, the yogi will acquire the knowledge of everything, as every sensible object and even thought is the result of this reaction. Then will he have seen the very foundation of his mind and it will be under his control.

'This meditative state is the highest state of existence. So long as there is desire, no real happiness can come. It is only the contemplative, witness-like study of objects that brings to us real enjoyment and happiness. The animal has its happiness in the senses, the man in his intellect, and the god in spiritual contemplation. It is only to the soul that has attained to this contemplative state that the world really becomes beautiful. To him who desires nothing, and does not mix himself up with them, the manifold changes of nature are one panorama of beauty and sublimity.'

16

RAJA YOGA IN A NUTSHELL

The following are a few points taken from a summarised translation of a section from *Kurma Purana*: There are two forms of Yogic concentration—*abhava yoga* and *maha yoga*. When oneself is meditated upon as a zero and bereft of quality, that is called *abhava yoga*. That in which one sees the Self as full of bliss and bereft of all impurities and one with God, is *maha yoga*.

Yama, niyama, pranayama, *pratyahara, dharana*, dhyana and samadhi are the steps of yoga. The disciplines of yoga are very much helped by the following practices: *niyama* or regular habits and observances; *tapas* or austerity; *svadhyaya* or vedic study; *santosha* or contentment; *saucha* or purity; and *Iswara-pranidhana* or worship of God. Repetition of the Vedas and sacred mantras purifies the *sattva* or stuff of the body-mind. Worship of God is by praise, remembrance of Him and devotion.

Pranayama is controlling the vital forces in one's body. It is divided into three parts—filling (*puraka*), restraining (*kumbhaka*) and emptying (*rechaka*). The *indriyas* or the organs of the senses, are going outwards. Bringing them under the control of the will is what is called *pratyahara* or gathering towards oneself. 'Fixing the mind on the lotus of the heart, or on the centre of the head, is what is called Dharana. Limited to one spot, making that spot the base, a particular kind of mental waves rises; these are not swallowed up by other kinds of waves, but by degrees become prominent, while all the others recede and finally disappear. Next the multiplicity of these waves gives place to unity and one wave only is left in the mind. This is Dhyana, meditation. When no basis is necessary, when the whole of the mind has become one wave, one-formedness, it is called Samadhi. Bereft of all help from places and centres, only the meaning of the thought is present. If the mind can be fixed on the centre for twelve seconds it will be a Dharana, twelve such Dharanas will be a Dhyana, and twelve such Dhyanas will be a Samadhi.'

Here are some samples of meditation prescribed: 'Imagine a lotus upon the top of the head, several inches up, with virtue as its centre, and knowledge as its stalk. The eight petals of the lotus are the eight powers of the Yogi. Inside, the stamens and pistils are renunciation. ... Inside of that lotus think of the Golden One, the Almighty, the Intangible, He whose name is Om, the Inexpressible, surrounded with effulgent light.' Another meditation is: 'Inside of that lotus think of the Golden

One, the Almighty, the Intangible, He whose name is Om, the Inexpressible, surrounded with effulgent light. Meditate on that. Another meditation is given. Think of a space in your heart, and in the midst of that space think that a flame is burning. Think of that flame as your own soul and inside the flame is another effulgent light, and that is the Soul of your soul, God. Meditate upon that in the heart. Chastity, non-injury, forgiving even the greatest enemy, truth, faith in the Lord, these are all different Vrittis. Be not afraid if you are not perfect in all of these; work, they will come. He who has given up all attachment, all fear, and all anger, he whose whole soul has gone unto the Lord, he who has taken refuge in the Lord, whose heart has become purified, with whatsoever desire he comes to the Lord, He will grant that to him. Therefore worship Him through knowledge, love, or renunciation.'

17

SUMMARY OF SWAMI VIVEKANANDA'S COMMENTARY ON PATANJALI'S YOGA SUTRAS

Section 1: Concentration: Its Spiritual Uses

17.1 WHAT IS YOGA? *VRITTIS* AND THEIR CONTROL

1-4[1] Yoga consists in restraining the mind stuff (*chitta*) from taking various modes of thought (*vrittis*), so that its background, the *purusha* or the centre of pure self-awareness, may be realised. The mind itself is not intelligent, even like the physical body, being a part of *prakriti* or nature, which is inert but dynamic. Being a product of *sattva* guna, the finest constituent of *prakriti*, the mind has, however, the refinement required to take on the self-conscious luminosity of the *purusha* by proximity, and thereby appear intelligent, though in itself it is not. As an aspect of dynamic *prakriti*, mind has the capacity to express itself as various movements or

---

1   The numbers given are of the *Yoga Sutras* of Patanjali.

modes (*vrittis*). Even when agitated by these various modes, the *chitta* (mind-stuff) reflects the consciousness of the spirit (*purusha*), but just as the agitated water of a reservoir prevents the revelation of the bottom of the reservoir, the *purusha*, whose light forms the background of these modes or *vrittis*, is Himself hidden by them, and what is seen of Him is only His reflection in an indistinguishably mixed up condition with the movement and colouring of the mind.

In perception, the *chitta* functions in a fourfold way. Its most external function is as the senses (*indriyas*) whose function is to establish contact with the objects. The *indriyas* convey the impulse to the concerned brain centre or the organ and from the organ it passes on to the mind (*manas*) and the *buddhi* (determinative faculty) and the *ahamkara* (the I-sense or individuation). The I-sense reacts to the stimulation, and perception as a self-conscious experience takes place. This complex process of the mind-stuff (*chitta*) through its varied functions as *ahamkara*, *manas*, and *indriyas*, resulting in awareness of objects, is called a mental mode or *vritti*.

Now the *chitta* is always like a highly agitated sea, disturbed by innumerable waves in the form of *vrittis*. Until all these *vrittis* are brought under control and the *chitta* rendered calm and unruffled, the distinctiveness of the spirit (*purusha*) from *prakriti* (matter or body-mind) cannot be realised. Till then the spirit will be under the false notion that He is body-mind. The fundamental purpose of yoga is therefore described negatively as the elimination of these *vrittis*, which means positively the revelation of the *purusha* on the mental modes being suppressed. The *purusha* then recognises His distinctiveness. He rests in His own nature as pure awareness and is no longer identified with the agitations of *Chitta*. That is the state of perfect samadhi.

17.2 THE FIVE KINDS OF *VRITTIS*

5-11 There are five kinds of mental *vrittis*, some of them painful and some pleasant. These are right knowledge (*pramana*), false cognition (*viparyaya*), fancy (*vikalpa*), sleep (*nidra*) and memory (*smriti*).

(1) *Pramana* or right knowledge is what is sanctioned by the three kinds of proof, namely sense perception, inference and competent authority. Supersensuous facts cannot be directly seen or inferred. They are experienced only by *aptas*. *Aptas* are highly evolved persons with the capacity to see supersensuous facts, and it is their evidence that is usually recorded in scriptures. Though these facts cannot be perceived or inferred, they can be realised by all, as the power of supersensuous perception can be developed by any one. In regard to right knowledge, the knowledge gained by one means will not contradict the others. It will only supplement them. (2) False cognitions (*viparyayas*) are false experi-

ences. They are no doubt experienced, but due to defects in the organs of perception, difficulties of situation, or wrong methods employed, the knowledge conveyed will be distorted or wrong. (3) In *vikalpa* (fancy or imaginative mental activity), there may be total or partial absence of factuality in respect of some experience or thought. 'Hare's horn' is an example of the total absence of factuality of an idea. In some others the experience is mainly subjective and not factual. (4) Sleep (*nidra*), though a negative experience has none the less to be classed as a mental mode, for it engulfs the whole mind in darkness, of which we have a memory afterwards. (5) Memory (*smriti*) can be the result of all the other mental modifications described earlier. Experiences leave an impression in the mind, and when these take shape, it is memory. It is said memories can be of two kinds. First there are memories that have become identical with the mind and are forgotten in waking. They appear as dreams. Perhaps what is called the subconscious and unconscious mind by the modern psychologists also can be included in it. The more superficial experiences which are remembered as memory form the second type; these can be recalled in waking life.

Now the control of all these five mental modes or modifications, which cause pleasure, pain, ignorance and delusion, is necessary to attain to the state of samadhi.

17.3 THE MEANS OF OVERCOMING
VRITTIS: *ABHYASA* AND *VAIRAGYA*

12-16 Practice (*abhyasa*) and *vairagya* (dispassionate-
ness) are the main requisites for subduing the *vrittis*
and attaining samadhi. Continuous effort to prevent
the rise of these *vrittis* through the practice of certain
disciplines, to be mentioned hereafter, is called *abhyasa*.
The practice should not be sporadic, but should be
undergone regularly and for long, with great faith and
devotion to the *Yoga Sastra*, its tradition and its teachers.
The human mind is a bundle of impressions left by our
actions. They become habits through repetitions. Constant repetition makes anything a habit and a second
nature. The various tendencies in the mind which generate these *vrittis* are counteracted by the new tendencies
the aspirant generates by his practice, regularly and for
long, with great faith and devotion. Sporadic practice
without the last mentioned conditions is no good.

Vairagya (dispassion), the second means of controlling the *vrittis*, is the disinclination of the mind for objects of the senses, accompanied with strong attraction
or aspiration for the spirit. We cultivate attraction for
objects from our previous experience of them and from
reports about them from others. This attraction is overcome in two ways: (1) by developing the power of discrimination. By reflecting on their injurious effect on

us, and on how they drag us to the life of suffering in the world, a sort of repugnance can be developed. This is *vitrishna*, or absence of attraction. (2) But this has to go hand in hand with a great attraction (*vasikara*) for the spirit. The more one's aspiration for the spirit, the less becomes the attraction for other objects. And when real knowledge of *purusha* arises, all aspects of *prakriti*, in their entirety, with all its riches, pleasures, ambitions, etc. become an absolute triviality. A man of real *vairagya* feels no attraction for objects of senses even when put in their midst. This *vairagya* of the highest order is equal to knowledge.

17.4 SAMADHIS OF DIFFERENT TYPES

17-18. Attainment of samadhi in which the *purusha* is intuited is the goal of yoga. It is now described in its different aspects. Samadhi comes under two main heads—*samprajnata* and *asamprajnata*. The first may be described as cognitive trance (or trance with object) and the second as supra-cognitive trance (trance without an object). The *samprajnata* or cognitive trance does not give freedom but only control over the various aspects of nature and therefore of powers pertaining to them. The various aspects of nature are the objects of concentration in this kind of samadhi. It is classified into four varieties. First when a gross element is the object of concentration the samadhi is called *savitarka*—questioning the elements. In the deeper state of it, when the element is taken out of space and time and concentrated upon by itself, the process is called *nirvitarka*. When the *tanmatra* or the subtle state of the gross element is meditated upon as in space and time, it is called *savichara*, i.e., with discrimination. When in the same meditation space and time are eliminated, it is called *nirvichara*, or without discrimination, homogeneous. The next stage is when the element is given up as the object, and meditation is done on the interior organs of perception, the *indriyas*. Meditation on the *indriya* bereft of rajas and tamas is called *sananda* or the blissful samadhi. When the mind itself becomes the object of concentration and the *sattva* state of the ego alone remains, but differentiated from all other objects, it is called *sasmita samadhi*. An aspirant who has attained to this is called 'bereft of body'. He no longer identifies himself with the gross body, but maintains his individuality with a subtle body and at the end of the cycle will become *prakriti-lina*, dissolved in *prakriti*. He is still away from the realisation as the *purusha* or free spirit. Such *purushas* come again in creative cycles as higher beings with control over nature.

Distinguished from these is the perfect *asamprajnata samadhi*, or supra-cognitive state of awareness without any object. This is accomplished by making the mind a vacuum, eliminating every form of object, and thereby, of all *vrittis*. Immediately one is able to do this, one is free, but though the process may look easy, it is the most difficult of all achievements. Unless the aspirant has extreme detachment and very strong aspiration, he will be overcome by tamas, dullness, in his attempt at this meditation. While he is only overcome by sleep, which is one of the *vrittis*, he will be under the false notion that he has made the mind a vacuum. But in a qualified person persisting in *asamprajnata samadhi*, all the tendencies of the mind, bad as also good, dissolve when samadhi becomes seedless. The mind itself is thereby dissolved. It may be questioned: without the mind what type of enlightenment can be had? The answer is that the knowledge got through the mind is inferior and is of limited things. It occupies an intermediate stage between the absolute dullness of matter and pure 'intuitive' awareness without object, which samadhi gives. In that pure intuitive awareness man knows himself as spirit. 'Then the man will know that he had neither birth nor death, nor need for heaven or earth. He will know that he neither came nor went, it was nature which was moving, and that movement was reflected upon the soul.'

The centre of intelligence or the *purusha*, who attains to supreme renunciation and, as a consequence, isolation from *prakriti* through knowledge or samadhi, passes out of the sway of *prakriti* and attains *kaivalya*.

Those who have reached the highest level of *samprajnata samadhi* and have only some good tendencies in them like doing good to suffering *jivas*, become *prakriti-lina* or absorbed in *prakriti*. They retain a subtle ego sense and in due time become devas or intelligent powers identified with aspects of *prakriti*, and controlling the functions of *prakriti*. Samkhya metaphysics, which is identical with that of yoga, does not accept one Universal Being as a creator-preserver God, as in their view *prakriti* and karma tendencies are enough to explain the world. But they admit this kind of *purushas* who become devas and govern creative activity.

The followers of the yoga system however accept a God, who is distinct from all *purushas*, and is the Teacher of all teachers.

17.5 WHO ATTAINS SAMADHI? AND HOW?

19-22. While samadhi is the result of long and strenuous practice as far as ordinary aspirants are concerned, it comes naturally to those who are *prakriti-linas*. *Prakriti-linas*, as already stated, are those accomplished yogins who are dissolved in *prakriti* but yet retain their ego sense based on some noble desires and therefore await another suitable embodiment. They do not require much spiritual practice, as they are already accomplished. But others have to strive in various ways, practising the prescribed disciplines assiduously. Success in the practice of samadhi will depend on the individual's fitness, that is, his endowment in respect of faith, energy, memory, concentration, discrimination and renunciation. The last point is to be stressed specially. Unless a person has the moral and physical maturity, he cannot do strenuous practice. Continence is most essential, and continence cannot be practised successfully unless the man has great spiritual aspiration and strength of discriminative intelligence. Swamiji has pointed out in other places that energetic practice of pranayama and high forms of meditation will adversely affect the brain and nervous system on incontinent persons, because of their unfitness to stand the strain.

So energetic practice with quick success in view has always to be moderated with the sense of one's capacity. For the vast majority of people, whose capacity is very ordinary, slow and steady practice will be better. So it is said in the 22nd aphorism that success differs according as the means adopted are mild, moderate or intense. This classification, besides being an exhortation, is also a caution to the aspirant against the hazard of practice without an assessment of his capacity and qualification. It also implies that patience is needed, as a long time will be required for the fruition of one's practices, if one's qualifications are not high.

17.6 THE PLACE OF GOD AND DEVOTION TO HIM

23-29. While renunciation and practice have in a general way been stated as the cause of spiritual illumination, other disciplines, which may be considered either as included in them or as supplementary to them, are also mentioned. The practice of devotion to God is first mentioned, thus making raja yoga almost identical with bhakti yoga. In the Samkhya metaphysics, on which the yoga system of Patanjali is based, there is no God. It says that 'there is no God. It says that there can be no God of this universe, because if there were one, He must be a soul, and a soul must be either bound or free. How can the soul that is bound by nature, or controlled by nature, create? It is itself a slave. On the other hand, why should the Soul that is free create and manipulate all these things? It has no desires, so it cannot have any need to create. Secondly, it says the theory of God is an unnecessary one; nature explains all. What is the use of any God? But Kapila teaches that there are many souls, who, though nearly attaining perfection, fall short because they cannot perfectly renounce all powers. Their minds for a time merge in nature, to re-emerge as its masters. Such gods there are. We shall all become such gods, and, according to the Sankhyas, the God spoken of in the Vedas really means one of these free souls. Beyond them there is not an eternally free and blessed

Creator of the universe. On the other hand, the Yogis say, "Not so, there is a God; there is one Soul separate from all other souls, and He is the eternal Master of all creation, the ever free, the Teacher of all teachers." '

The yoga system however does not give much stress on the creative function of God, as in the bhakti texts; matter and spirits are independent of Him. He is more a teacher and redeemer of souls and not so much a creator or a will controlling creation. He is a special spirit (*purusha-visesha*) who has never been affected by the bondages of the other *purushas* like misery (*klesa*), action, work and its results and desires (*asa*). Limited knowledge which ordinary *purushas* have, implies un-limited knowledge as a background, for it is by a hazy contrast between these two that one's notion of limited knowledge arises at all. Both these notions, of limited knowledge on the one hand and of unlimited know-ledge on the other, go together like the two ends of a line. So, if there are *purushas* with limited knowledge, then there must be a *purusha* answering to the notion of unlimited knowledge also, and that is *Iswara*. Besides, all knowledge has to come through teachers. There have been many great teachers, but they, being only ordinary *purushas*, have been in bondage once, and their cap-acity to teach is limited. They must have also received their knowledge from someone earlier. Thus there is a necessity to accept an original teacher, unlimited by time, from whom knowledge has come in succession to others. That original teacher, the teacher of teachers, is *Iswara* according to the yogis.

Devotion to *Iswara* (*Iswara-pranidhana*) means essentially contemplation on Him with the accompaniment of repetition of the mantra Om. The sacred symbol Om is considered His manifesting word (*vachaka*). Some translate *vachaka* as 'indicating word'. The connection between *Iswara* and Om is considered inherent and not conventional, as in the case of other sounds and objects denoted by words. Even the relation between ordinary objects and their names is not as conventional as one ordinarily supposes. According to the philosophy of sound, every thought or idea is possible only with a corresponding sound symbol. So, in spite of the variation in the sound symbols used to indicate objects, there is some naturalness in the relation between the idea of an entity and its name. So, indirectly though, even the varying sound symbols in different languages have an inherent relation with their object.

But the relation between Om and *Iswara* is much more natural, as Om is the only perfect sound to indicate the perfect being. Other names of God are more conventional, but not Om. In fact Om includes them all. 'But there must be a generalization among all these words, some substratum, some common ground of all these symbols, and that which is the common symbol will be the best, and will really represent them all. ... Om (Aum) is such a sound, the basis of all sounds. The first letter, *A*, is the root sound, the key, pronounced without touching any part of the tongue or palate; *M* represents the last sound in the series, being produced by the closed lips, and the *U* rolls from the very root to the end of the sounding board of the mouth. Thus, Om represents the whole phenomena of sound-producing. As such, it must be the natural symbol, the matrix of all the various sounds.' Besides, by usage through millennia, this word has come to represent every possible idea of the Supreme Being. For example, the English word God conveys only a very limited idea of God, and if one wants to express expanded ideas of Him, you have to add adjectives as personal God, impersonal God, etc. But Om, being used in India by every sect and school of thought, has come to mean any and every conception of the Supreme Being. It deserves therefore to be accepted by all to be the most appropriate *vachaka* (manifesting word) for God.

The sound symbol Om must be repeated continuously, accompanied with meditation on its meaning, namely the Supreme Being. Repetition is necessary to strengthen our spiritual tendencies, just as association with holy men is needed to strengthen these tendencies by putting us in touch with the Supreme Being. Continuous repetition with concentration produces what may be called molecular vibration, which will persist even when there is no external repetition with effort. Repetition and contemplation of the meaning can go on simultaneously.

By the realisation of *Iswara* who is free from the bondage of *prakriti*, the *purusha*, who is 'spirit under illusion', comes to recognise that he too is a free spirit like *Iswara*. The recognition is born of the introspective power generated by repetition and meditation. From that introspective power, the aspirant also overcomes the obstacles to yoga.

17.7 OBSTACLES TO YOGA

30-41. The obstacles (*antaraya*) to yoga are listed as follows: (1) ill-health, (2) feeling of helplessness, (3) doubt or vacillation, (4) lack of enthusiasm, (5) stupor due to dullness of body and mind, (6) hankering for sense enjoyments, (7) false perceptions, (8) not reaching the state of communion, and (9) falling away from it when attained. When the aspirant is faced with these obstacles and fails to get concentration, his mind will be agitated by grief, irritation, trembling due to nervous shaking, and irregular and uncontrolled breathing.

In such situations, in order to get over these depressive and unhelpful moods, one is asked to do *eka tatvab-hyasa,* dwelling on a single object. According to some, that single object is God, and according to others, any material object. As any single object will not suit all, different objects for dwelling upon are given. The mind can be pacified by dwelling on some noble qualities related to suitable subjects. For example, one may dwell on friendship towards one happy; pity for one unhappy; joy for one good; and indifference to one evil.

Another method suggested is exhaling and drawing in deep breaths, keeping the breath out and in for very short periods. The process should be done consciously unlike in our usual breathing, which is done unconsciously. Conscious breathing means that the mind should be watching the breath.

For those whose faith is flagging are suggested certain concentrations yielding quick results. If the mind is concentrated on the tip of the nose for a few days, wonderful perfumes will be experienced; if on the root of the tongue, sweet sounds will be heard: if at the tip of the tongue, agreeable flavours will be got; if on the palate, peculiar tastes will be felt. Such experiences are helpful sometimes to give faith in yoga and thus clear one's doubt about it.

Another meditation suggested is on an effulgent light in the centre of one's heart, imagined as a lotus. Imagine the petals of the lotus drooping downwards, and as the breath is thrown out, imagine the petals as turned up with the effulgent light within. Or, one can meditate on the heart of a saint who is free from all attachment to sense objects. Or, if one has got some spiritual experiences in dream, one can meditate on that, taking the dream as real. Or, one can meditate on any idea, or scenery or experience that has an ennobling effect on one. All these will make the disturbing *vrittis*, the modes of the mind, weak, and the mind becomes capable of concentrating on anything, from the very minute to the biggest of things.

When the mind gains this concentratedness, it becomes like a crystal which gets the identical colour as the object near which it is placed. This state of identification with the object is called the state of coalescence (*samapatti* or samadhi). There are three entities in a perception—the object that is perceived, the instruments like the senses with which perception takes place, and the perceiver, the *purusha*. The mind can concentrate on any of these three and get coalescence with it, as a crystal with the colour of a flower before it.

17.8 THE SUPPRESSION OF *VRITTIS*

42-51. *Savitarka samadhi* (samadhi with question) is now described. In this the duality between the subject and the object is kept up, which is the result of mixing up sound, meaning and knowledge. Sound or the word is the external vibration. The nerve currents that carry it inward is the meaning. When it is carried to the *chitta*, the wave that comes as reaction is the knowledge of the object. These three are mixed up, i.e., not distinguished in the *savitarka samadhi*, and besides, the distinction between the subject and object is maintained.

By long practice, this confusion between external vibration (sound), the inner nerve vibration (the meaning) and the reaction of the *chitta* (knowledge of the object) are distinguished from one another, and the meditating mind shines out as the object alone, all other memories being forgotten or effaced. Such a state of identification is called *nirvitarka samadhi* (samadhi without question).

The expression *savitarka* and *nirvitarka* are applied when the concentration is directed to gross objects like atoms and things made by their combination. When the concentration is directed to subtle objects, the terms *savichara* and *nirvichara* are used. Subtle object means all categories from *tanmatra*s up to *prakriti* itself. The yoga system of Patanjali accepts the Samkhya cosmology. In brief these subtle categories, in ascending order of subtlety from the gross elements onwards, are—the subtle elements (*tanmatras*), the organs (*indriyas*), the mind (*manas*), egoism (*ahamkara*), the collective intellect (*mahat*), and *prakriti* (nature or matter), also called as *pradhana* and *avyakta*, with its three constituents of sattva, rajas and tamas. All the succeeding categories are evolutes of *prakriti* or nature, and are material substances devoid of consciousness in themselves. Separate from all this is *purusha*, the centre of pure consciousness, by association with whom the evolutes of *prakriti* get a reflected consciousness. Now *savichara* and *nirvichara* samadhis can be with reference to all these subtle objects or their combinations. In the former, because the object is concentrated within the limitation of space and time, the distinction between the seer, instrument and object is kept up, while in the latter, the mind becomes identified with the object and shines as the object.

All these samadhis are directed towards objects and keep up the distinction between the subject and the object. They are called *sabija*, with seed, because they do not fully destroy all the effects of past actions, and therefore do not liberate the *purusha* from rebirth. But when *savichara* samadhi is persisted in for long, it purifies the mind, and frees it from the dullness of tamas and the agitation of rajas, and makes it *ritambhara*, filled with the light of Truth. This means that the aspirant develops the power of intuition, by means of which he can directly apprehend spiritual truth, for understanding which ordinary men depend on scriptures and on reasoning about the data given by scriptures.

The samadhi produced by such concentration generates so powerful a *vritti*, wave or modification, that it suppresses all the modifications caused by the impressions of earlier experiences which have been coming out and disturbing the mind whenever it attempted to concentrate. But so long as the mind has any modification at all, the *purusha* is not released. So yoga is described as the total elimination of all *vrittis* or mental modifications. Therefore this residual modification, which eliminates all others, also has to go ultimately. This is effected in the following way: by the practice of *savichara samadhi*, *chitta* is no more directed to external objects, and its outward-going tendency has ceased completely. Further, by contemplating on its own source-principle like *prakriti* for long, it gets dissolved in it, and even the residual mental modifications disappear leaving the *purusha* free from all bondage. Thus *samprajnata samadhi* in its deeper levels ends in *asamprajnata samadhi* (objectless awareness) and this in turn ends in *kaivalya* or aloofness of the spirit from matter.

Until this state of *kaivalya* or aloofness is attained, one cannot perceive the soul, because it has got mingled with nature, with the mind and the body. This mingling takes place because different waves in the *chitta* (*vrittis*) rise and cover the soul, and we see only a little reflection of the soul through these waves. Getting identified with these waves, the soul, or rather the reflection of the soul, thinks it is angry, happy, suffering, joyous and so on. But really its nature is unaffected; there has only been a mixture of effects due to proximity. So, only when all the waves, including the last one of *nirodha* (restraint) of all other waves, subsides, that the samadhi becomes *nirbija* (seedless) and *asamprajnata* in the true sense. 'The Soul is manifested just as It is, in Its own glory. Then alone we know that the Soul is not a compound; It is the only eternal simple in the universe, and as such, It cannot be born, It cannot die; It is immortal, indestructible, the ever-living essence of intelligence.'

Section 2: Concentration: Its Practice

17.9 KRIYA YOGA

1-2. Practice of samadhi can be done only in an advanced state of spiritual development. The mind has to be prepared for it. That preliminary preparation is called *kriya yoga*. Literally the term means 'working towards Yoga.'

The preparatory discipline called *kriya yoga* is three-fold—austerity, scriptural study, and practice of devotion to God. Austerity or *tapas* does not mean torturing the body or doing anything that weakens the faculties of the mind. It means controlling the mind and the senses and directing their energies to higher purposes. Soft living, incontinence, gluttony and other forms of sensual indulgences are to be avoided. Study or *svadhyaya* means here the study of scriptural and devotional texts that will strengthen one's spiritual inclination. Controversial or argumentative side of study has not much relevance at this stage. If one is intellectual, one should have passed through it already. Conclusions or *siddhanta* is the more relevant part of scriptural study. Argument at this stage is a waste of energy. Intellect is a poor aid. In yoga, the effort is to rise above the senses and the intellect to intuition. Repetition of mantras is also an aid in this. Devotion to God includes discharge of all one's duties as offering to God, besides practising love and surrender to Him. Thus all the preliminary disciplines of bhakti yoga are also brought within the scope of the yoga discipline.

This *kriya yoga* is very important, because it is only through the long practice of it that what are called the *klesas* or pain-bearing obstructions to the practice of yoga can be overcome, and one gradually gains the fitness to practise samadhi. There are men who take to yoga disciplines with the expectation of quick results. But such practice will be quite ineffective, if one has not become fit by the proper mode of life.

17.10 *KLESAS* OR PAIN-BEARING OBSTRUCTIONS

3-11. The *klesas* are five: ignorance (*avidya*), egoism (*asmita*), attachment (*raga*), aversion (*dvesha*) and clinging to life (*abhinivesa*). Of all these, ignorance is the most fundamental, being the cause of all the other afflictions. They can exist in an attenuated or developed form. When they are stimulated by loose living and indiscriminate contacts, they become stimulated, or 'expanded'. They are then difficult to control. It is to prevent this situation that austere living and other aids are recommended as a means for controlling *klesas* or pain-bearing afflictions.

Ignorance is the sense of identification of the Self or the spirit with the non-self or body, which is impermanent, impure and subject to pain. By such identification these defects of the not-self are attributed to the Self. *Asmita* or egoism consists in identification of oneself with the instruments of perception and their functions and experiences. The instruments of the spirit are the *chitta* or the mind stuff, the *buddhi* or the determinative faculty, the *manas* or the mind, and the senses. The complex of these is the instrument with which the *purusha* experiences the *prakriti*. Identification with this complex as the 'I' is *asmita*. Attachment or *raga* is the hankering to have repetition of the experiences that one has found pleasurable from previous experiences. *Dvesha* or aversion is the attitude towards unpleasant experiences. This may take the form of fear, anxiety or anger, according to the nature of the situation. *Abhinivesa* is the subtle and almost unconquerable instinctive drives from within, especially the will-to-live that is present in all living beings from the animals to the most learned men. This will-to-live is the self-preservation instinct present in all beings. An instinct is an inborn, untaught and almost irresistible reaction, as of a duckling to dip into a pond of water at the sight of it. The will-to-live or the self-preservation instinct is the most fundamental instinct. Other inborn drives like sexuality, acquisitiveness, pugnacity, gregariousness, etc., can come under *abhinivesa* or instinctive tendency 'flowing through its own nature and established even in the learned' In our ordinary experience we find that if we do anything repeatedly for long, it becomes automatic, or in other words, instinctive. So it can be argued that what are now accepted as instinctive tendencies like the will-to-live, etc., have become so through repeated experience. So it is held that it is the experience of life and death in countless embodiments of the past that present themselves now as instinctive tendencies. Their presence is used as an argument in support of reincarnation. Repeated experiences leave *samskaras* or subtle tendencies in the *chitta*. They work in a subtle fashion from the subconscious layers of the mind. It is comparatively easy to recognise and control the gross waves (*vrittis*) of the mind, but not so these subtle movements. To control these mental waves we have to get down below to their causes, objectify them and non-identify ourselves from them; for, when we become angry, we are anger for the time being, and through identification, anger has got complete control over us. So if we are to control such undesirable *vrittis* or modes of the mind, they have to be recognised early in their fine causes and counteracted by objectivisation, or by bringing opposite tendencies to work on them. But such meditative process can put down only the gross manifestation of the tendency as a mental wave. The root impressions that cause them will continue in the *chitta*. These can be effaced only when the *chitta*, the medium of their recording, is resolved into its causal category, *ahamkara* or the I-sense.

17.11 BONDAGE AND LIBERATION

12-27. All actions that man performs leave their effect on the mind of the doer. These are called *samskaras*, and they fructify in due time as enjoyments and suffering, in the future life of the doer. Irrespective of their nature all these karmic effects have their root in the 'pain-bearing obstructions' (*klesas*). From the point of view of the yogi, even good karma bringing on enjoyments are to be looked upon as pain-bearing, because their effects, though pleasure-giving from a worldly point of view, are really a cause of suffering for the yogi, as they too stand in the way of his subduing all the mental *vrittis* and attaining release. Thus, all effects of karmas, classed as adverse or good according to the sufferings or enjoyments they yield, are alike evil for the yogi for two reasons: (1) The so-called pleasurable enjoyments are sure to end at one time or other and the resulting

deprivation will cause intense suffering, (2) Irrespective of the nature of their effects, karmas cause further
births and deaths, which are in themselves suffering. So,
every kind of work, good or evil, is a cause of suffering,
and the *klesas*, the pain-bearing obstructions described
before, form their reservoir.

The misery that is in store, or is yet to take shape
through new karma, can be avoided unlike what has
already been experienced or is being experienced. This
avoidance can be effected by the isolation of the seer
from the seen, the subject from the object. The seer or
the subject is the *purusha* who is the centre of intelligence without any activity. The seen or the object is the
prakriti, nature with all its evolutes, out of which the
body-mind of man and the mighty universe, which he experiences through that body-mind, have evolved. *Prakriti*
is constituted of the three elements of sattva (light), rajas
(dynamism) and tamas (inertia). Its first evolute is *mahat*
(the Great Entity); from that, *ahamkara* (Individuation);
from that, *manas* (mind-stuff), *buddhi* (intellect), sense
organs (*indriyas*), subtle elements (*tanmatras*) and gross
elements (*bhutas*). The whole universe, including the
body and the mind of living beings, is made by the combination of these categories. *Prakriti* and its products are
dynamic but not intelligent or self-conscious. *Buddhi* and
the mind too are inert; intelligence expressed by them is
only the reflection of the intelligence of *purusha*, the seer.

The whole purpose of the evolution of *prakriti* is
to give experiences to the *purusha*, the seer, and thus
bring Him out of entanglement in it. The *purusha*, who
by nature is all intelligence, purity, bliss and freedom,
has, due to proximity with *prakriti*, forgotten His own
identity and got the colouring of *prakriti* as a crystal is
coloured by a red flower close to it. He has not lost His
nature, but by identification with *prakriti*, has forgotten it and become one with the movements of *prakriti*
through proximity, lending at the same time the light
of His intelligence to the segment of *prakriti* with which
He is identified. He is identified with that segment of
prakriti which forms the complex of body-mind that
serves as the instrument for Himself to contact the external environment provided by *prakriti*. The body-mind
really belongs to the world of the seen and is therefore
separate from the seer or the *purusha*. But proximity
leads to identification. All the movements and modifications of the body-mind through contact with nature outside, are taken and enjoyed by the *purusha* as
His. This is involvement in the travails of *samsara*, the
cause of His being in ignorance. Even in this state of
involvement, the sense of one's freedom is ever bubbling
up, but simultaneously the shackles of nature's bondage also weigh heavily. Freedom can be fully realised
only by recognising the separateness of the seer from
the seen. Recognition remedies *samsara*, because the

purusha has not lost His self-conscious and blissful nature even in that state but is only labouring under false identification due to proximity with *prakriti*.

Ignorance, which is the cause of identification between *prakriti* and *purusha*, is dispelled by the practice of discriminative understanding continuously. The successful practice of discrimination gives the following seven-fold conviction: (1) that one has come to a correct understanding of the cause of bondage and that further external quest for theoretical understanding is uncalled for; (2) that one has adopted the correct means for overcoming those causes of bondage and suffering; (3) that one has by the practice of *samprajnata samadhi* experienced the elimination of these causes; (4) that all duties have been accomplished through direct communion and nothing remains to be done; (5) that all difficulties on the way and vacillations of the mind have fallen away, just as a stone falls down from the top of a hill to the valley and will not come up again; (6) that the *chitta* itself is melting away into its cause whenever one desires so; and (7) that the spirit has all along been aloof and alone and that neither the mind nor the body was ever joined to it. These latter were working their own way and the *purusha*, through infatuation, got identified by proximity, but not by contact. This recognition secures for the *purusha* absolute aloofness from the movements of *prakriti*. The yogi then recognises himself to be inherently pure, perfect, immortal and blessed, untouched by any sorrow.

The whole purpose of the functioning of nature is to present various experiences to the *purusha* and help him ultimately understand that he has never been connected actually with *prakriti*, but only identified with it through ignorance. When the separation is recognised, the *purusha* realises His essential nature of aloofness from *prakriti*. Now according to the Samkhya *philosophy*, which is in many respects common to yoga also, the *purushas* are numberless. So the question arises as to what happens to nature when a *purusha* attains aloofness. The answer is that ignorance is destroyed only for that one *purusha* and he alone attains aloofness. The function of *prakriti* continues as before for all the other *purushas* who are still in ignorance.

17.12 THE EIGHT STEPS OF YOGA

28-55. The description given till now is about the theory of yoga and the highest reaches of its attainment. But so long as the impurities are not destroyed, the discriminative intelligence, which destroys the entanglement of the *purushas* with *prakriti*, cannot be strengthened. It will be strengthened and rendered effective only if the theoretical understanding of yoga is supported by the practice of the eight-limbed yoga discipline. These eight limbs of yoga are now described. They are *yama*, *niyama*, asana, pranayama, *pratyahara*, *dharana*, dhyana and samadhi.

Yama (absolute restraint) consists of: non-killing, truthfulness, non-exploitation, continence and non-acceptance of gifts. To put it in positive language, it means benevolence, integrity, honesty, celibacy, and self-dependence. These are to be practised by all aspirants without distinction of time, place or status. In that sense they are absolute.

Niyamas (relative restraints) are: cleanliness including internal purification, contentment, austerity, scriptural study, and worship of God. They are called relative in the sense that according to time, place and circumstance there can be variations in period devoted, modes adopted, etc., in their practice.

Cruelty, jealousy, hatred, sexuality, greed, dishonesty, etc., are obstructions to yoga. They create adverse impressions which confer fruits of a painful nature through repeated rebirths. By constant contemplation of their evil consequences and by meditating on their opposite qualities of a virtuous nature, the mind must be made steady in the practice of *yama* and *niyama*.

The ideals of perfection attained through the practice of *yama* and *niyama* are described. In the presence of one who is perfect in ahimsa, others give up mutual antagonism. In the case of one who is established in truth (*satya*), his words become true and his very thoughts will fructify. *Brahmacharya* (avoidance of sexuality in thought, word and deed without any sense of repression) enhances the person's stamina, physically, mentally and intellectually. Sex energy gets converted into *ojas*, which fortifies his brain and nervous system to stand the strain of the yoga discipline. *Ojas* is food to the psychic being of man as physical food is to the body. Without *brahmacharya* strenuous spiritual practice is dangerous. The words and deeds of a man with great *ojas* exert a far-reaching influence on the life of his fellow-beings. By being established in *aparigraha* (non-dependence), a yogi comes to have knowledge of his past lives. It. gives him a vivid idea of the recurring nature of life and death, and strengthens his resolve to get out of that cycle and be free.

Now the fruits of *niyama* are described. *Saucha* (cleanliness outside and inside) gives a man a sense of uncleanliness of the body as such and produces a feeling of abhorrence for it. It gives also *sattva-suddhi*, purity of mind, which generates cheerfulness, concentration and alertness of the mind so necessary for spiritual practice. The idea that a spiritual man must be morose is a total misconception. Moroseness is a sign of tamas. A true yogi always brims with a sense of blissful joyousness. Contentment gives true happiness. *Tapas* (austere living) destroys impurity and adds to the vigour and keenness of the mind and the intellect. True *tapas* is not flesh-torturing, but a life of self-restraint and concentration. *Swadhyaya*, which includes scriptural study and repetition of the mantra, brings about the realisation of the chosen deity. Surrendering everything to God in devotion can give even samadhi. Thus Patanjali emphasises the important place of devotion to God in the practice of yoga.

The step that follows is posture or asana. Control of asana means gaining mastery over sitting for a long time in a straight, erect posture in which the spine, neck and head are in one line. Firmness of seat means that while so sitting, one does not feel the body at all, unlike in other positions. The body will also feel refreshed when the position is changed afterwards. Without mastery of such a position, pranayama and meditation are not possible because of movements and nervous disturbances. Mastery of a firm sitting position is helped by thinking of an infinite existence like the sky or the ocean. One who has mastered the seat is not disturbed by dualities of heat and cold caused by climatic changes, or by pains and aches in the body resulting from sitting.

The next step is pranayama consisting in controlling the motions of inhalation and exhalation. The reader is referred to the earlier chapter on prana. Prana is not breath, but the sum total of the cosmic energy, a part of which is functioning in each body. The most obvious manifestation of it is the movement of the lungs, caused by the prana drawing in the breath. The object of pranayama is to control this movement of the lungs, and through that, gain control of the prana working in the whole system. There are three kinds of pranayama described. Drawing in the air slowly through one nostril and, after retaining it for a short prescribed period of time, breathing it out through the other nostril. The process is repeated for the prescribed number of times. The inhaling process is called *puraka*, the exhaling, *rechaka*. When breath is suspended without taking in or throwing out air, the suspended state is called *kumbhaka*. The result of pranayama is *udghata*, rousing of kundalini. These three processes of pranayama are performed by the yogi with conscious effort. The fourth type of pranayama is the *kumbhaka* attained naturally without any effort by one who has been practising long. It is specially attended with reflection, which is not present in the ordinary *kumbhaka*.[2]

---

2   The practice of pranayama appears attractive because of its apparent precision. But it has to be remembered that unless a person has the moral fitness included in the disciplines of *yama* and *niyama*, unless one's heart, lungs and nervous system are sound, unless one has a strong spiritual aspiration and unless one has the guidance of an accomplished teacher, it is very risky for people to practise pranayama as a major discipline. In the absence of these conditions and qualifications, for the vast majority of aspirants it is better to be satisfied with a simplified form of pranayama. Fairly long breaths may be taken and expelled

Pranayama purifies the *chitta* (mind-stuff). *Chitta* is made of elements of sattva, but the influence of rajas and tamas makes it an imperfect instrument for meditation. Pranayama removes this covering of the *chitta*. The mind then becomes fit for the next step of *dharana*. *Dharana* is established when the organs leave their objects and take the form of the mind-stuff. The organs are distinct aspects of the mind. In sense contact they get a stimulation from outside and carry it to the mind-stuff, and it is the mind-stuff that takes the form of the object perceived. If the organs are prevented from going out, they will rest in the mind stuff, which will therefore be free from modifications. This restraining of the mind-stuff from taking shapes is *pratyahara* or obstruction. When a yogi is established in *pratyahara*, he obtains perfect control of the body and mind. There are two kinds of organs—the five organs of knowledge and the five organs of action. When all these are under perfect control, one will experience a sense of bless-

without retention. Breathing should be done consciously, i.e., bestowing attention on the respiratory process. Doing this a few times will make breathing rhythmic and also narrow the field of attention. As for *kumbhaka*, it can come even naturally if devotion to the Supreme Being is practised, accompanied with fervent meditation. Sri Ramakrishna says that love of God can produce *kumbhaka*, rousing of *kundalini* and samadhi. In this Patanjali also seems to agree when he says that *Iswarapranidhana* is one of the principal ways of controlling the *vrittis* (modes) of the mind and attaining *samadhi—Publisher.*

edness. The next three steps are described in the next
chapter.

Section 3: Powers

17.13 SAMYAMA

1-15. The sixth step of yoga is *dharana* or concentration. It is the state when the abstracted mind is kept
steadily on an object within the body or outside. Any
centre in the body like the navel, the heart, tip of the
nose, head, etc., or forms of Gods like Vishnu, Siva,
Devi, etc., can be made the object of concentration.
When *dharana* becomes steady and the mind does not
go to any other object, that state of mind is called dhyana or meditation. The distinction between the two is
that in *dharana* there is effort to fix the mind. In *dharana*
the mind can slip away but not in dhyana. When the
mind remains in the object spontaneously without effort for a considerable length of time, that is dhyana,
the seventh step of yoga.

Dhyana continued successfully culminates in the
next step samadhi, when the seer feels identified with
the object, overcomes the barrier of its form, and grasps
its meaning unexpressed in any form. In dhyana the distinction between the object and the conceptual understanding of the object remains. This is overcome in
samadhi when the object as such is known through

identification with it, overcoming the barrier of the form. Knowledge gained in this way is unclouded by the passions, prejudices and conceptual framework of the individual mind, and as such it has to be valued as more fundamental than anything that mere perception with our senses can give.

When *dharana*, dhyana and samadhi are practised with regard to one object, it is called a *samyama*. *Samyama* gives an unobstructed and unclouded understanding of an object by at-one-ment with it. The form of the thing vanishes, and only the meaning remains in the mind.

Samyama is the great instrument of the yogin. Its practice must be from lower forms to higher forms. For example, *savitarka* form of concentration should be perfected before the *nirvitarka* form is taken, and so also *savichara* before *nirvichara*. In the same way gross objects should be taken before finer objects are attempted; for examples *bhutas* before *tanmatras*, concrete forms before the ideas behind them, the objects before *indriyas* etc. One should go slow and not be in great haste.

There are three stages in the mastery of *samyama*. In the first stage concentration produces a *vritti* by controlling the other modifications of the mind only imperfectly. The other *vrittis* are only held back but not suppressed. In the second stage these are completely suppressed by the *vritti* of concentration, and that alone stands. This state of undisturbed concentration is samadhi. By practice it becomes an unbroken wave of consciousness in which the sense of time is lost. Past and present meet in a sense of continuing present. At this stage *samyama* is said to have become natural and under the control of the aspirant.

17.14 POWERS

(16-50) The power of concentration obtained through *samyama* opens the way for gaining various kinds of occult powers. By making *samyama* on various objects, these powers are gained. By making *samyama* on the three-fold changes in the impressions of the mind (*samskaras*), past and future are known. The threefold changes are changes in form, changes in time and changes in state. If by *samyama* on a sound, one is able to distinguish between its form, the meaning and the object it denotes, unlike in the ordinary perception in which these are confused and mixed up, one will have a knowledge of the meaning of all sounds made by man as well as animals. By *samyama* on the signs in another's body, a yogi can know his mind, and by another *samyama* on his mind, all its contents. By *samyama*, the yogi can separate the form of his body from its essence, obstruct the visibility of the form, and thus make himself invisible to others while actually present in a place. By making *samyama* on his own karma and through portents, a yogi can know the time of his own death. By *samyama* on virtues, the yogi can excel in them. By *samyama* on the strength of an elephant, immense strength is gained. By *samyama* on the light in the heart, the yogi gets perception of highly refined objects as also of very distant objects even beyond mountain barriers. The following are some of the other *samyamas* and their results. By making *samyama* on the sun, knowledge of the world; on the moon, knowledge of clusters of stars; on the pole-star, knowledge of the movements of the stars; on the navel, knowledge of the constitution of the body; on the hollow of the throat, cessation of hunger; on the nerve called *kurma*, fixity of the body; on the light emanating from the top of the head, the sight of siddhas and other heavenly beings; on the heart, knowledge of the mind.

Even without *samyama* all these higher powers come naturally to one who has *pratibha*, a spontaneous enlightenment from purity. When the *buddhi*, the sattva element in one, is free from the influence of I-sense, it becomes capable of reflecting the pure light of the *purusha*. One who is always established in such a *vritti* or mental modification is said to have attained *pratibha*, and for such a one, super-sensual hearing, touching, seeing, smelling, hearing, etc. become natural without any *samyama*. But if the yogi is attracted by these, he cannot come to the highest state of knowledge, which is

born only with the total rejection of the manifestations
of *prakriti* as worthless. In fact *prakriti* and its powers
are functioning only to give experience to the *purusha*,
and when he is satisfied with these experiences and is
no longer attracted by them, then alone can he reject
prakriti totally and become 'self-centred' or gain aloofness (*kaivalya*): All *vrittis* then subside, including the
sattva. So all the powers are obstacles to samadhi, and
a real yogi has to reject them all.

A yogi who has come to the experience of the distinctiveness of the *purusha* from *prakriti*, can enter another
body or revive another body with the help of his mind,
which has become one with the universal mind. He can
loosen himself from the nerve currents of his own body
and work through that of another. By conquering *udana*,
a nerve current, he can make himself lighter and float
in water or walk on thorns. By conquering the nerve
current *samana*, he can bring out flashes of light from
his body. By making *samyama* on the relation between
the ear and akasha, he gets supernormal hearing and
can hear sounds spoken even miles away. Akasa being
the material of the body, the yogi by making *samyama*
on this relation, can become light like akasha and travel
anywhere through the skies. The yogi can exclude his
ego-sense from the mind. The mental modification that
arises in the absence of egoism is called *akalpita*, or 'not
imaginative' i.e. real, and also 'great disembodiedness'

(*mahavideha*). With this *samyama* the removal of all coverings of the light of knowledge takes place, and darkness and ignorance vanish. By making *samyama* first on the gross and then on the subtle aspect of elements (the live *bhutas* and their *tanmatras*), the yogi gets control over elements and is endowed with the 'eight powers' like making oneself minute as a particle, as huge as a mountain, as heavy as earth, as light as air, etc. He can go anywhere, he can rule everywhere, and conquer everything. A lion will be like a lamb before him; and all his desires will be fulfilled. He attains great beauty, strength and stamina. By making *samyama* on the sense organs (*indriyas*) with reference to their tendency to go towards objects and illumine them, as also on their association with egoism, their relation to gunas, and their contribution to the experience of the soul, these organs are conquered. From this the yogi gains such powers as making rapid movements of the body like the mind, functioning of the organ independent of the body, and conquest of nature. By *samyama* on the distinction between *sattva* (*buddhi*) and the *purusha*, the yogi gains mastery of all nature and universal knowledge.

17.15 POWERS AS OBSTACLES TO YOGA

(51-56) If the yogi's power of discrimination is well-established and he cares for liberation alone, he gains intense dispassion (*vairagya*) even for this state of all-power and all-knowledge that nature offers as the ultimate prize. If he can discard even this prize, then alone he will be established in *kaivalya*, the state of independence and aloofness from *prakriti*. It requires strong discrimination to realise that these powers are only temptations and bondages. Besides the powers, there are celestial beings also who try to tempt the yogi with celestial nymphs, power and enjoyments, as he passes through their spheres in the course of these developments. These celestial beings are fallen yogis, that is, those whose renunciation was not strong enough to overcome the powers that yoga gives, and consequently leaving the royal road, having got trapped in blind alleys. The remedy against this is the strengthening of the power of discrimination. This is done by *samyama* on a moment (*kshana* or smallest unit of time) with consciousness of its succession, and not in combination with other *kshanas* as a long unit of time. A *kshana* is the smallest particle of time taken by one *paramanu* (atom) to move from its space to the one next to it. Such a particle in its distinctiveness as moving to the space of the next, and not as a succession of moments put together as a period of time, is the object of concentration. This gives the sense of ephemerality of everything in *prakriti*.

When this power of discrimination is strengthened, man finds that everything in nature is a compound and is impermanent, and as such cannot be the *purusha* who is the only simple, timeless entity. This heightened power of discrimination is called saving knowledge (*tarakam*). This knowledge is powerful enough to grasp the whole of *prakriti* in all its states without any distinction of past, present and future, because there is no succession in the awareness that this knowledge gives. The *buddhi*, which is also called sattva, is ordinarily a mixture of purity and impurity. Being of the sattvika nature, it is pure, but due to the association of all the modifications of *prakriti* it becomes impure. By the discriminative process mentioned, it becomes devoid of all *vrittis* born of material contacts and impressions. Then it reflects only the purity of the *purusha* and becomes pure like Him. By the similarity of the purity of the reflecting *buddhi* with that of the *purusha*, *kaivalya* or aloofness of the *purusha* is realised; for then the *buddhi* reflects only the unqualified essence of the *purusha*.

Thus it will be seen that though the *siddhis* are mentioned, they have no direct reference to *kaivalya*, which the yoga philosophy has in view. It is a non-essential part of yoga just as the *karma-kanda* is of the knowledge part of the *Veda*. Besides, it is contrary to the outlook that has to be developed by *yama* and *niyama*; for, *siddhis* can be had only from *samyama* done with the particular object or power in view. The trend of the *Yoga Sutras* is therefore to minimise the importance of *siddhis* and put emphasis on the development of discrimination and knowledge, which alone can yield *kaivalya*. At the most, the *siddhis* can only be a test of the aspirant's spirit of renunciation.

Section 4: Independence

17.16 WHEN *SIDDHIS* ARE RELEVANT

(1-8) While the *siddhis* mentioned before may come to one in the course of the practice of samadhi, they can also manifest in some at birth due to practice of yoga in a previous birth, and in some others by the use of certain medicinal elixirs (*aushadhi*), by incantation (mantra), and mortification (*tapas*). These latter developments are not indications of spiritual advancement, but only temporary episodes caused by a break-through of the obstructions in the way of manifestation of powers inherent in *prakriti*. All powers are inherent in nature, and not in the medicinal herb or the incantations. These are only instruments in causing temporary break-through in the obstructions to the manifestation of the powers of *prakriti*. It is just like a cultivator cutting open a blind and allowing the water already there to flow out. Such exhibition of power is temporary and may result in harm to their possessor. It is very well known how addiction to drugs for bringing on delightful mystic experiences, ultimately makes nervous wrecks of men.

Powers are therefore never a sign of spiritual great-
ness. They have significance only when they appear as
the side-effects during the practice of samadhi. In one
practising samadhi they are spontaneous manifestations
and are accompanied by non-attachment and absence
of desires. For, he has passed through earlier disciplines
like *sama* and *dama*, which have established him at a
high moral level. He has also overcome the five *klesas*
or pain-bearing obstructions. Being without desires
for enjoyments, he is not affected by the meritorious
results of his good actions, and having given up all
evil, he never performs bad actions. He has therefore no
karmic, residue. Hence it is only the persons practising
samadhi through yogic discipline that are on the way
to emancipation, and not the others who get powers by
medicines, incantations or mortifications. For, the latter are full of desires, and the bondage of karma is on
them as in the case of all subject to desires.

17.17 CONQUEST OF DESIRES

(8-13) The sway of desires is endless, because it is
based on the eternal craving for happiness. Therefore
left to nature, the process, consisting of desires prompting action, actions creating new impressions and these
begetting fresh actions, will go on without end. Desires
are kept alive by the following factors: (a) their cause

consisting in action; (b) their results consisting in the
subtle impressions they leave; (c) their support in the
mind-stuff which retains the impressions in subtle form
indefinitely; (d) and lastly there are the external objects,
the contact with which stimulate these impressions and
bring them out as gross desires ending in actions for
their fulfilment. This vicious circle can be broken only
by getting rid of these four factors that help the sur-
vival of desires.

17.18 OBJECTS ARE REAL

(14-16) All that we experience exist eternally in subtle
state in the gunas. When a segment of it is manifested
to the mind, we call the manifested state the present,
and the subtle and unmanifested states we call the past
and the future. All existence is eternal; there is nothing
coming into being from non-existence and going into
non-existence. There are the two states, the manifested
and the unmanifested, which are mistakenly called orig-
ination and destruction. The gunas of *prakriti* are the
constituent substance of all that exists as past, present,
and future, and as the change involved is of one stuff
and is co-ordinated by succession, there is a sense of
their unity. The gunas in the course of their modification manifest as organs of apprehension like hearing,
seeing, etc., and they also manifest as objects—as parti-

cles of air, fire, etc., and their combinations into atoms and into bigger entities produced with atoms. Objects of apprehension are not mere mental ideas, but have their autonomous existence. If not, different people cannot apprehend the same thing as identical, in spite of variations in their impressions. Both mind and objects are two series of expressions of the gunas of *prakriti*, the former being the subject or the seer, and the latter the object or the seen. Even where there is no mind to know an object, the object exists. Knowing and not knowing objects, only means their colouring or not colouring the mind, and not their being produced by the mind.

Thus the universe is both mental and material. The material objects form one series of molecules in constant change, and the mental another such series of fast changing substances which seem to apprehend the other series. Both are fast changing, and if each of them seems to be a unity, it is due to the harmonious continuity of the change. Both mind and matter are however layers of the same substance, the gunas of *prakriti*, and if they are distinguished, it is because of the difference in the speed and subtlety of their movement.

17.19 THE *PURUSHA* AND HIS ISOLATION

(17-23) The mind itself is thus a product of *prakriti*, and just like other products of it, an object seen by a

seer. It is also inert and without intelligence in itself.
It may be coloured by the objects, but it cannot in itself be conscious of that colouring. This consciousness
comes from the *purusha*, the pure principle of awareness, whose form it takes by proximity, and becomes
capable of being aware of external objects with which
it is coloured. But in itself it is not self-conscious, as is
proved by the fact that when it is aware of its objects, it
is not aware of itself. A self-conscious entity will be simultaneously aware of itself and of anything it illumines.
The *purusha* alone is thus the self-conscious principle
who lends His self-luminous awareness to the mind, by
virtue of which the mind becomes capable of seeing the
objects reflecting on it. In its own nature, mind is inert
and an object to a seer like everything else in *prakriti*.

The mind is thus like a screen which is identified with
the self-conscious light of the *purusha*, and reveals for
the *purusha* all the objects with which it is coloured. This
colouring of the mind is not only by external objects
but by all the subtle impressions of the experiences it
had passed through, leaving residual impressions on the
mind. When the mind is disturbed by these impressions,
it is lashed into disturbing *vrittis* (waves of thought), just
as by contact with objects. They are to be controlled
just like the overcoming of the *klesas* (impediments) described in Chapter II (Sutras 3-13). The impressions are
ultimately overcome only when *chitta*, their base, is re-

solved in its cause, *asmita*, the I-sense. Meditation alone cannot destroy them, although their gross manifestation can be controlled by early observation and effort. They have to be tackled when they first manifest. One has to be aware of them and objectify them as foreign to the Self, before they seize the self completely.

It is only when the mind is comparatively freed from the colouring of objects and impressions, that it can reflect the full Self-consciousness of the *purusha* and have that power of discrimination through which the yogi understands that the mind is not the *purusha*. When this discrimination is established, the *purusha* gets isolation (*kaivalya*) from *prakriti* (nature and its manifestations). Discrimination gives clearness of vision and puts an end to the mistaken notion of taking the mind to be the Atman. 'The veil drops from the eyes, and we see things as they are. We find that nature is a compound, and is showing the panorama for the Purusha, who is the witness; that nature is not the Lord, that all the combinations of nature are simply for the sake of showing these phenomena to the Purusha, the enthroned king within. When discrimination comes by long practice, fear ceases, and the mind attains isolation.'

'When the Yogi has attained to this discrimination, all the powers mentioned in the last chapter come to him, but the true Yogi rejects them all.' One who cannot do this, but succumbs to their charm, has not attained to the climax of discrimination, the supreme *vairagya* (non-attachment) which alone can reveal all the charm of *prakriti* as trivial. To one who rejects all these *siddhis* which are his for the asking, comes a peculiar knowledge, a particular light, called the *dharmamegha*, 'the cloud of virtue'. All the great prophets of the world whom history has recorded, had this. They had found the whole foundation of knowledge in themselves. Truth to them had become real. Peace and calmness and perfect purity became their own nature after they had given up the vanities of power. When 'the cloud of virtue' has come, then there is no more danger of falling, nothing can drag the yogi down. Nor will there be evil for him, nor more pains. Knowledge itself is there, its covering is gone. Knowledge becoming infinite, the knowable becomes small. The whole universe, with all its objects of knowledge, becomes as nothing before the *purusha*.

At this stage *prakriti* has completed the purpose of its evolution into various categories and their combinations. The purpose is to present before the *purusha* her various formations for Him to enjoy. This enjoyment is had by the *purusha* through identification with the modifications of *prakriti* which provides Him with mind as instrument to enjoy and objects as material for enjoyment. When, through the development of discrimination, the *purusha* has realised his distinctiveness from the mind and thereby attained isolation from *prakriti*,

prakriti has fulfilled her function and retires as far as that *purusha* is concerned. Evolution, which consists in the succession of moments recognised at the end of a period with the distinction of past, present and future, ceases for the *purusha* that has realised omnipresence. Everything becomes an eternal present, the past and the future being lost. Time stands controlled and all knowledge is there in an instant. Everything is known in a flash.

This is the state of kaivalya, where nature with the gunas, having lost all purpose, involves in the reverse order and becomes latent in the purusha. It is the establishment of the power of consciousness in its own nature without involvement in prakriti. 'Nature's task is done, this unselfish task which our sweet nurse, nature, had imposed upon herself. She gently took the self-forgetting soul by the hand, as it were, and showed him all the experiences in the universe, all manifestations, bringing him higher and higher through various bodies, till his lost glory came back, and he remembered his own nature. Then the kind mother went back the same way she came, for others who also have lost their way in the trackless desert of life. And thus is she working, without beginning and without end. And thus through pleasure and pain, through good and evil, the infinite river of souls is flowing into the ocean of perfection, of self-realisation.'

PART 3: BHAKTI YOGA

Section 1: Apara-bhakti or Preparatory Devotion

18

WHAT IS BHAKTI?

18.1 BHAKTI AND *JNANA*—THEIR RELATION

'Bhakti-Yoga is a real, genuine search after the Lord, a search beginning, continuing, and ending in love.' It 'has been the one constant theme of our sages.' Even commentators on the Vyasa-sutras, who are evidently advocates of knowledge (jnana), have something very suggestive to say about it.

The difference between knowledge (jnana) and love (bhakti) which some people imagine does not exist in reality. The jnanis hold bhakti to be an instrument of liberation; the bhaktas look upon it both as the instrument and the thing to be attained. 'To my mind this is a distinction without much difference. In fact, Bhakti, when used as an instrument, really means a lower form of worship, and the higher form becomes inseparable from the lower form of realisation at a later stage. Each seems to lay a great stress upon his own peculiar method of worship, forgetting that with perfect love true knowledge is bound to come even unsought, and that from perfect knowledge true love is inseparable.'

18.2 FANATICISM THE GREAT PITFALL
OF BHAKTI SCHOOLS

The one great advantage of bhakti is that it is the easiest and the most natural way to reach the great divine end in view. Its great disadvantage is that in its lower forms it oftentimes degenerates into hideous fanaticism. The reason for this is that to many an undeveloped mind the singleness of attachment to one object or ideal (*nishtha*) is possible only by hating the ideals and personalities adored by others. Their love is like the canine instinct of guarding the master's property against all intrusion; but while the dog can recognise the master in any garb, the fanatic cannot!

The best safeguard against this tendency is to develop a noble character in which knowledge, love and yoga are harmoniously fused. For attaining to the heights of spiritual consummation, it is better that the bird of the aspirant is equipped for the flight with the two wings of knowledge and love, and with the tail of yoga as rudder for steering.

18.3 DEFINITION OF BHAKTI
BY DIFFERENT TEACHERS

" 'The loving wife meditates on her loving husband" here also a kind of eager and continuous remembrance is meant. This is devotion according to Shankara.'

Constant remembrance is denoted by the word 'bhakti', says Ramanuja. This constant remembrance means the unbroken flow of the mind towards an object, as when oil is poured from one vessel to another. Such remembrance, when exalted, assumes the same form as seeing, that is, becomes as vivid and real as in seeing, although in ordinary sense *'seeing'* and *'remembering'* are different. Constant remembering, repeated worship and spiritual understanding (*jnana*) are identical in import. That is why scriptures speak of *smriti* (remembrance) as the means of liberation. For, he who has this constant remembrance of Him, is dear to Him, is 'desired by the Supreme Atman', and is consequently helped by the Lord to attain to Himself. Such are the views of Ramanuja on the subject.

The teacher of yoga Patanjali, recognises *Iswarapranidhana* as a means for spiritual enlightenment. His commentator Bhoja defines *pranidhana* as that sort of bhakti in which, without seeking results such as sense enjoyments, all works are dedicated to the Teacher of Teachers; and Vyasa, another commentator, calls *pranidhana* as that form of bhakti by which the mercy of the supreme Lord comes to the yogi and blesses him.

Sandilya, yet another teacher of the bhakti school, defines it as intense love of God. He uses the word *anurakti* for love. 'Anu, after, and Rakti, attachment.' It is therefore attachment that comes after the knowledge that He is the Supreme Being. For, love directed to Him alone is bhakti. All other beings, except God, the *Bhagavan*, are subject to karma, and they are not worthy of worship by a bhakta.

'The best definition is, however, that given by the king of Bhaktas, Prahlāda: "That deathless love which the ignorant have for the fleeting objects of the senses— as I keep meditating on Thee—may not that love slip away from my heart!" '

19

THE PHILOSOPHY OF *ISWARA*

19.1 THE ABSOLUTE AND *ISWARA*

Generally the definitions given of *Iswara* (God) describe Him as personal. ' "From whom is the birth, continuation and dissolution of the universe,' " is one definition. 'He is Iswara—"the Eternal, the Pure, the Ever-Free, the Almighty, the All-Knowing, the All-Merciful, the Teacher of all teachers" '—is another definition. And above all is the definition: " 'He the Lord is, of His own nature, inexpressible Love.' "

Are there then two Gods—the negatively described *sat-chid-ananda*, the Existence-Knowledge-Bliss of the philosopher, and this God of love of the bhaktas? 'No, it is the same Sat-chit-ananda who is also the God of Love, the impersonal and personal in one.' Only the Brahman, as the unity or Absolute, is too much of an abstraction to be loved and worshipped; so the bhakta chooses the relative aspect of Brahman, that is *Iswara*, as his object of love and worship. *Iswara* is the highest manifestation of the Absolute Reality, or in other words, the highest possible reading of the Absolute by the human mind. Creation is eternal and so also is *Iswara*.

19.2 THIS DOES NOT MAKE *ISWARA* LOWER OR UNREAL

When it is said that *Iswara* is the highest reading of the Absolute by the human mind, it should be clearly understood that it does not in the least imply any idea of *Iswara* being an inferior reality or a product of anthropomorphic subjectivism. 'True it is that we cannot have any idea of Brahman which is not anthropomorphic, but is it not equally true of everything we know? The greatest psychologist the world has ever known, Bhagavan Kapila, demonstrated ages ago that human consciousness is one of the elements in the make-up of all the objects of our perception and conception, internal as well as external. Beginning with our bodies and going up to *Iswara*, we may see that every object of our perception is this consciousness plus something else, whatever that may be; and this unavoidable mixture is what we ordinarily think of as reality. Indeed it is, and ever will be, all of the reality that is possible for the human mind to know. Therefore to say that *Ishvara* is unreal, because He is anthropomorphic, is sheer nonsense. It sounds very much like the occidental squabble on idealism and realism, which fearful-looking quarrel has for its foundation a mere play on the word "real". The idea of Ishvara covers all the ground ever denoted and connoted by the word real'

19.3 DIFFERENCE OF
THE BHAKTI SCHOOLS ON THIS POINT

It should, however, be noted that the philosophers of the pure bhakti school are not in full agreement with this interpretation of *Iswara* as the highest reading of the Absolute by the human mind. This comes out clearly in their discussion of the condition of the liberated souls. In discussing Vyasa's *Sutras* on this subject, all bhakti schools agree that such liberated souls, freed from all the limitations of ignorance, get infinite power, knowledge and bliss. But they retain their distinction from *Iswara* eternally, because *Iswara* is distinguished from them by the essential attribute of the power of creation and direction of the world systems. No liberated *jiva* can have this, as he is subordinate to *Iswara* in all conditions of ignorance and liberation.

Acharya Ramanuja's, however, is a philosophy which accepts the unity of all existence, but to all practical purposes its implication is dualistic. The liberated one attains to extreme sameness and all his desires are realised. This means only that such liberated ones, from whom all that veils his true nature has been removed, only enjoy the unobstructed perception of Brahman, but do not possess the power of ruling the universe. For, ruling the universe is the uncommon attribute, the differentia, which distinguishes *Iswara* from everything, including the liberated *jivas*. So although the system of Ramanuja admits the unity of the total, within that totality of existence, there are, according to him, eternal differences. Therefore, being dualistic to all practical purposes, it is very easy for Ramanuja to keep the distinction between the personal soul and the personal God very clear.

19.4 A POSSIBLE RECONCILIATION

Sankara's Advaita philosophy of *Iswara* as the highest reading of the Absolute by the human mind, has already been described. There is thus a clear-cut difference in the conception of *Iswara* between the bhakti and the Advaitic schools. A reconciliation however can be attempted.[3] The main ideas connected with this have

---

3   The difficulty in the full reconciliation of the positions of pure Advaitism and the bhakti schools arises from the differences in their metaphysical and ethical outlooks. The points involved in the two outlooks may thus be stated. (1) The bhakti schools will not make a distinction between God and the absolute, if the absolute means something higher than God. According to them God is the highest Being, and not a conceptual view of something higher, be it an absolute or anything else. (2) For the bhakti schools, God and the absolute are thus the same. This highest

already been stated, under the heading, 'The Philosophy of *Iswara*,' Besides, it has to be remembered that to keep their separateness or be one with Brahman, is within the choice of the *jivas*. 'Those who aspire to retain their individual mind even after liberation and to remain distinct will have ample opportunity of realising their aspirations and enjoying the blessing of the qualified Brahman. These are they who have been spoken of in the *Bhagavata Purana* thus, "O king, such are the glorious qualities of the Lord that the sages whose only pleasure is in the Self, and from whom all fetters have fallen off, even they love the Omnipresent with a love

---

being, God, is for them personal. Those bhakti philosophers who admit impersonality consider it as a lower manifestation of the personal, thus reversing the situation. (3) According to them, bhakti is the highest consummation for a *jiva*. bhakti means service of God as total involvement in Him. So a distinction based on a loving relationship between *jiva* and *Iswara* is to be admitted in the nature of things and accepted as final. (4) Many of the bhakti schools admit complete absorption of consciousness in God, as described in the above paragraphs. But their interpretation of it differs. For them consciousness is an attribute of Being, unlike for the pure Advaitin, for whom pure being and pure consciousness are identical. So, for the Advaitin, when the *jiva* and *Iswara* become one in consciousness, they become identical in Being or Entity too. But for the bhakti schools, even when consciousness gets absorbed in God as in the case of the *go' is* and other devotees, it is only in attribute they become one, as the light of a tiny lamp with sunlight, but their entities remain separate always. All these differences are due to differences in the metaphysical outlook.—Publisher.

that is for His love's sake.' " (*Samkhyas* also have a similar theory that some liberated *jivas* become absorbed in
prakriti to come out in a next creation as the Governors
of new world systems). Even these *mukta souls* cannot
be equal to God, though their will might be one with
His. But 'Those who attain to that state where there is
neither creation, nor created, nor creator, where there
is neither knower, nor knowable, nor knowledge, where
there is neither *I*, nor *thou*, nor *he*, where there is neither
subject, nor object, nor relation, "there, who is seen by
whom?"—such persons have gone beyond everything to
"where words cannot go nor mind", gone to that which
the Shrutis declare as "Not this, not this"; but for those
who cannot, or will not reach this state, there will inev-
itably remain the triune vision of the one undifferentiated Brahman as nature, soul, and the interpenetrating
sustainer of both—Ishvara. So, when Prahlāda forgot
himself, he found neither the universe nor its cause;
all was to him one Infinite, undifferentiated by name
and form; but as soon as he remembered that he was
Prahlada, there was the universe before him and with it
the Lord of the universe—"the Repository of an infinite
number of blessed qualities". So it was with the blessed
Gopis. So long as they had lost sense of their own personal identity and individuality, they were all Krishnas,
and when they began again to think of Him as the One
to be worshipped, then they were Gopis again.'

'Bhakti, then, can be directed towards Brahman, only in His personal aspect.' The above philosophy of *Iswara* 'maintains all the hopes and aspirations of the dualist intact, and at the same time propounds its own solution of the problem in consonance with the high destiny of divine humanity.'

20

AIDS TO BHAKTI

20.1 SPIRITUAL REALISATION: THE AIM OF BHAKTI YOGA

The true *bhakta* does not care for these philosophical details. He soon goes beyond these turbulent and hazy regions of reason to the calmness and clarity of realisation. He no more reasons and believes, he almost perceives. Not only that; *bhaktas* have not been wanting who have maintained that it (bhakti or serving God in truth and in spirit) is higher than even moksha—liberation.

This kind of whole-hearted devotion or service of God is also of the highest utility. There is, however, a very large section of people who would not care for bhakti or concede that it is the highest value. Of them it is said: 'To men, therefore, who never rise higher than eating, drinking, begetting progeny, and dying, the only gain is in sense enjoyments; and they must wait and go through many more births and reincarnations to learn to feel even the faintest necessity for anything higher.

But those to whom the eternal interests of the soul are of much higher value than the fleeting interests of this mundane life, to whom the gratification of the senses is but like the thoughtless play of the baby, to them God and the love of God form the highest and the only utility of human existence.'

20.2 THE PLACE OF SYMBOLS, RITUALS, ETC., IN PREPARATORY BHAKTI DISCIPLINE

Bhakti yoga is divided into two parts—*gauni* or preparatory, and *para* or the supreme. In the preparatory stage of bhakti man needs the help of many mythological and symbological aids, and these features, which form the characteristic of all the great religions, are natural developments out of the mind of man. They have arisen because of the extreme need that man has of these for his spiritual development in its early stages. Spiritual giants have grown only in religions that have a rich mythology and ritualism.

There are dry types of religion, which in the name of their curious conceptions of rationalism, eschew all these values, poetical, artistic and sublime. They forget that it is these values that give 'a firm grasp to the infant mind tottering in its Godward way ... in their ignorant and superstitious conceptions of truth try to drive away all that is life-giving, all that furnishes the formative material to the spiritual plant growing in the human soul ... they will soon find that all that is left to them is but an empty shell, a contentless frame of words and sophistry with perhaps a little flavour of a kind of social scavengering or the so-called spirit of reform.'

The vast mass of people who advocate the above-mentioned type of religion and religious living are conscious or unconscious materialists. The end and aim of their lives here and hereafter is only enjoyment. They are like people who consider 'street-cleaning and scavengering, intended for the material comfort of man is, according to them, the be-all and end-all of human existence; and the sooner the followers of this curious mixture of ignorance and fanaticism come out in their true colours and join, as they well deserve to do, the ranks of atheists and materialists, the better will it be for the world.'

Realisation is the aim of bhakti yoga and not mere frothy sentimental talk about the welfare of all with no intention to put it into practice.

20.3 THE NEED OF A GURU

The quickening of the spiritual impulse in man cannot be achieved merely through books. From books only our intellect derives development, but not our spiritual susceptibilities. There is, however, some value even in such intellectual stimulation. For, it may in course of time result in the awakening of a real thirst for religion.

It is not true that a high order of intellectual development signifies a proportionate development on the spiritual side. Many scholars are deluded into such a belief.

The quickening of the spiritual impulse can come only from another soul that is itself deeply spiritual or enlightened. 'The person from whose soul such impulse comes is called the Guru—the teacher; and the person to whose soul the impulse is conveyed is called the Shishya—the student.' This, however, implies that the guru must possess that power of transmitting the impulse, and that the soul to which it is transmitted is fit to receive it. 'The seed must be a living seed, and the field must be ready ploughed; and when both these conditions are fulfilled, a wonderful growth of genuine religion takes place.'

20.4 WHEN A TRUE GURU BECOMES AVAILABLE

Some of the dangers attendant on the spiritual path may be listed thus: (1) A man may mistake a mood of spiritual quest that comes on him as a result of some bereavement, disappointment or allied happenings to be a permanent conversion. But this may turn out to be temporary and pass of soon, and he may soon become his own merry self. 'as long as these momentary emotions are thus mistaken, that continuous, real craving of the soul for religion will not come.' And until this real craving comes, 'we shall not find the true transmitter.' There will be no spiritual development under these conditions, and men will complain, saying that all spiritual philosophy is an exercise in futility. But it will be more profitable for them to look into themselves than get into this complaining mood; and in the vast majority of cases it will be found that we have no real craving and we are not fit for receiving the truth. (2) There are still greater dangers with regard to the transmitter of truth, the guru. 'There are many who, though immersed in ignorance, yet, in the pride of their hearts, fancy they know everything, and not only do not stop there, but offer to take others on their shoulders; and thus the blind leading the blind, both fall into the ditch. ... The world is full of these. Every one wants to be a teacher, every beggar wants to make a gift of a million dollars! Just as these beggars are ridiculous, so are these teachers.'

20.5 QUALIFICATIONS OF THE ASPIRANT AND THE TEACHER

The greatest teachers of the world are those high-souled persons in whom wisdom and truth shine like the sun, self-evident to all. Such persons are worshipped by men as manifestations of God.

But there are lesser kinds of teachers also, and the

true student must have the intuition and intelligence to judge them. If the aspirant has got genuine purity of life and real thirst after knowledge, an unremitting and continuous struggle, a constant grappling with the lower nature which will not stop until victory is achieved—such a student is bound to come to a real teacher and attain success and realisation.

Regarding the qualification of the teacher, he must *Srotriyo avrjino akamahato yo brahmavittamah* (one who is learned in the scripture, sinless, unpolluted by lust and a great knower of Brahman). Now '*Srotriyah*', ' "learned in scriptures" ' does not mean an expert in interpretation of texts, in epistemology, grammar, etc., of the scriptural passages, but one who embodies in himself the spirit of the scripture, one who lives the life inculcated by the scriptures. A scholar in scripture and its interpretation is like a leaf-counter in a mango garden, while he who lives the spirit of it is like a mango-eater therein.

The second condition is that a teacher must be sinless and unpolluted by lust (*avrjinah, akamahatah*). Secular subjects like mathematics can be studied from anyone who has an intellectual understanding of them, irrespective of what his character is. 'but in the spiritual sciences it is impossible from first to last that there can be any spiritual light in the soul that is impure. ... A vision of God or a glimpse of the beyond never comes until the soul is pure.' Hence regarding the teacher of religion we must see first what he is and then only what he says. The function of the teacher is indeed an affair of the transference of something and not one of mere stimulation of the existing intellectual or other faculties of the taught.

The third quality of a real teacher is that he is without any ulterior motive like money or fame. He must be motivated by pure love alone. 'God is love, and only he who has known God as love can be a teacher of godliness and God to man.'

Men who are not of the above nature but yet play the part of the Guru are a source of positive danger. In place of conveying goodness into the heart of their disciples, they may convey the wickedness that is within them.

20.6 RELATION OF THE TEACHER AND DISCIPLE

The eye opener of the aspirant in respect of the spiritual Truth is the teacher. Krishna says in the Bhagavata 'Acharyam ma vijaniyat—"Know the Guru to be Me." ' With the teacher, therefore, our relationship is the same as between an ancestor and his descendants. Without faith, humility, submission and veneration in our hearts towards the religious teacher, there cannot be any growth of religions in us. Gigantic spiritual men will grow only in such societies where this kind of reverence for the teacher is upheld and not where 'the religious teacher has become a mere lecturer, the teacher expecting his five dollars and the person taught expecting his brain to be filled with the teacher's words, and each going his own way after this much has been done. Under such circumstances spirituality becomes almost an unknown quantity. There is none to transmit it and none to have it transmitted to.'

'Religion, which is the highest knowledge and the highest wisdom, cannot be bought, nor can it be acquired from books. You may thrust your head into all the corners of the world, you may explore the Himalayas, the Alps, and the Caucasus, you may sound the bottom of the sea and pry into every nook of Tibet and the desert of Gobi, you will not find it anywhere until your heart is ready for receiving it and your teacher has come. And when that divinely appointed teacher comes, serve him with childlike confidence and simplicity, freely open your heart to his influence, and see in him God manifested. Those who come to seek truth with such a spirit of love and veneration, to them the Lord of Truth reveals the most wonderful things regarding truth, goodness, and beauty.'

21
INCARNATE TEACHERS
& INCARNATIONS

21.1 WORSHIP OF INCARNATIONS: ITS NEED

'Higher and nobler than all ordinary ones are another set of teachers, the Avatāras of Ishvara, in the world. They can transmit spirituality with a touch, even with a mere wish. The lowest and the most degraded characters become in one second saints at their command. They are the Teachers of all teachers, the highest manifestations of God through man. We cannot see God except through them. We cannot help worshipping them; and indeed they are the only ones whom we are bound to worship.' Man's effort to think of God as He is, neglecting these human manifestations and their worship, is one of the most thoughtless excursions into the realm of philosophical speculations. Some people pretend to be rationalists and seek to prove that all accounts of the avataras of God as man are merely fanciful accounts for the consumption of ignorant men. Such an attitude is born of ignorance and thoughtlessness.

If you ask them what their idea of God is, they will trot out big words like 'omnipotence,' 'omnipresence,' etc., but if you further ask them what they mean by these words, they will be found to have no idea of them beyond their spellings. They cannot formulate any idea of these concepts except through human nature, and they are no better in this respect than the man in the street who has not read a single book. The only difference between them is that the man in the street does not disturb the peace of the world while the big talkers 'creates disturbance and misery among mankind. ... So we cannot help seeing God as man, and, therefore, we are bound to worship Him as man.'

Two kinds of human beings do not worship God as man, the human brute who has no religion on the one hand, and on the other, the *paramahamsa* who has transcended human nature and to whom all nature has become his own Self, whose self has become one with God. 'Being between these two poles of existence, if any one tells you that he is not going to worship God as man, take kindly care of that man; he is, not to use any harsher term, an irresponsible talker; his religion is for unsound and empty brains.' 'God understands human failings and becomes man to do good to humanity. ... "When a huge tidal wave comes," says Bhagavan Shri Ramakrishna, "all the little brooks and ditches become full to the brim without any effort or consciousness on their own part; so when an Incarnation comes, a tidal wave of spirituality breaks upon the world, and people feel spirituality almost full in the air." '

21.2 GOD CAN BE WORSHIPPED ONLY IN HIS MANIFESTATIONS

'God cannot be worshipped; He is the immanent Being of the universe. It is only to His manifestation as man that we can pray. ... When these are thought of, these great ones, they manifest themselves in our souls, and they make us like unto them. ... But you must not mix up Christ or Buddha with hobgoblins flying through the air and all that sort of nonsense. ... The great strength of Christ is not in His miracles or His healing. Any fool could do those things. Fools can heal others, devils can heal others. I have seen horrible demoniacal men do wonderful miracles. They seem to manufacture fruits out of the earth. I have known fools and diabolical men tell the past, present, and future. I have seen fools heal at a glance, by the will, the most horrible diseases. These are powers, truly, but often demoniacal powers. The other is the spiritual power of Christ which will live and always has lived—an almighty, gigantic love, and the words of truth which He preached. The action of healing men at a glance is forgotten, but His saying, "Blessed are the pure in heart", that lives today. These words are a gigantic magazine of power—inexhaustible. So long as the human mind lasts, so long as the name of God is not forgotten, these words will roll on and on and never cease to be. These are the powers Jesus taught, and the powers He had. The power of purity; it is a definite power. So in worshipping Christ, in praying to Him, we must always remember what we are seeking. Not those foolish things of miraculous display, but the wonderful powers of the Spirit, which make man free, give him control over the whole of nature, take from him the badge of slavery, and show God unto him.'

22

THE PHILOSOPHY OF THE MANTRA

The ordinary siddha gurus transmit spiritual wisdom to disciples through mantras, certain sound symbols to be repeated and meditated upon. An understanding of the philosophy of mantras or sound symbols becomes therefore important.

Om' is the basic sound representing the sphota or the creative word or idea, into which the Supreme Being manifests in His creative role, first as hiranyagarbha (also called mahat) and then into the various forms of the world of creation. Om, the creative word (sphota), is called Sabda-Brahman (Sound-Brahman). The point to remember is that every manifested form experienced here has got a corresponding idea (called also as name or 'word', nama), and this idea precedes the form in the Cosmic Mind. Now the universal idea which is the sphota, including all ideas, is best represented by Om, because it is the most non-particularised and all-inclusive of sounds. 'Om and the Sphota are one. And as the

Sphota, being the finer side of the manifested universe, is nearer to God and is indeed that first manifestation of divine wisdom, this Om is truly symbolic of God. Again, just as the "One only" Brahman, the Akhanda-Sachchidānanda, the undivided Existence-Knowledge-Bliss, can be conceived by imperfect human souls only from particular standpoints and associated with particular qualities, so this universe, His body, has also to be thought of along the line of the thinker's mind. This direction of the worshipper's mind is guided by its prevailing elements or Tattvas. The result is that the same God will be seen in various manifestations as the possessor of various predominant qualities. ... Even as in the case of the least differentiated and the most universal symbol Om, thought and sound-symbol are seen to be inseparably associated with each other, so also this law of their inseparable association applies to the many differentiated views of God and the universe: each of them therefore must have a particular word-symbol to express it. These word-symbols, evolved out of the deepest spiritual perception of sages, symbolise and express, as nearly as possible the particular view of God and the universe they stand for.' These are the mantras, and they are all helpful in the practice of divine meditation and the acquisition of true knowledge.

22.2 THE EFFICACY OF THE MANTRA

'Such a name must come from a person to whom it
has descended through right succession. From Master
to disciple, the spiritual current has been coming from
ancient times, bearing its power. The person from whom
such a word comes is called a Guru, and the person to
whom it goes is called a Shishya, the disciple. When
the Word has been received in the regular way, and
when it has repeated, much advance has been made in
Bhakti Yoga.'

'The Mantra-Shāstris (upholders of the Mantra theory) believe that some words have been handed down
through a succession of teachers and disciples, and the
mere utterance of them will lead to some form of realisation. There are two different meanings of the word
Mantra-chaitanya. According to some, if you practise
the repetition of a certain Mantra, you will see the Ishta-
Devatā who is the object or deity of that Mantra. But
according to others, the word means that if you practise the repetition of a certain Mantra received from a
Guru not competent, you will have to perform certain
ceremonials by which that Mantra will become Chetana
or living, and then its repetition will be successful. Different Mantras, when they are thus 'living', show different signs, but the general sign is that one will be able
to repeat it for a long time without feeling any strain

and that his mind will very soon be concentrated. This is about the Tantrika Mantras.

From the time of the Vedas, two different opinions have been held about Mantras. Yāska and others say that the Vedas have meanings, but the ancient Mantra-shastris say that they have no meaning, and that their use consists only in uttering them in connection with certain sacrifices, when they will surely produce effect in the form of various material enjoyments or spiritual knowledge. The latter arises from the utterance of the Upanishads.'

23

IMAGE WORSHIP

Worship of God through a *pratika* means worshipping Him through a substitute, taking that substitute to be Brahman Himself. Thus in the *Upanishads* we find mind, akasha, sun, name, etc., taken as *pratikas* and invoked as Brahman. Another kind of *pratika* worshipped in *Tantras* and *Puranas* are *pitris* and devas. Various forms of ritualistic worship have been described to propitiate these.

Now worship of anything other than Brahman cannot generate bhakti and mukti. Such worship is at best idolatry. Though in no way sinful, it can at best yield the results accruing to it, but not bhakti and moksha. It is like ritualistic karma of the *Vedas*. Unless the worshipper views that *pratika* as an expression of Brahman and worships it as Brahman, it will not lead to bhakti and mukti.

This is true of *pratimas* also. A *pratima* is an image of a god or a saint. If the image stands only for the god or the saint, such worship will not lead to bhakti and mukti. But if it stands for the one God, that worship will bring both bhakti and mukti.

In every great religion, the worship of *pratikas* and *pratimas* has entered in some form or other. Muslims, while externally standing against image worship, use the graves of their saints and martyrs for worship. The Kaba is also holy for them. The Catholics use images freely. But in all these religions, such worship takes only the form of pure *pratika* worship without any idea of worshipping the one universal God through them, in other words, merely as acts of propitiation and not as help to the vision (*Drishtisaukaryam*) of God. Therefore they are at best like ritualistic karma and cannot produce bhakti or mukti.

23.2 UPANISHADIC *PRATIKAS* AND NATURE WORSHIP

The word pratika means coming towards, 'nearing'. In a devotional sense it means an object taken as a symbolic substitute for Brahman on the basis of some remarkable quality in it, in respect of which it is supposed to resemble Brahman. It is taken for worship and meditation on the basis of scriptural injunction and on the acceptance of the fact that it is a manifestation of Brahman or that Brahman indwells it. Thus in the upasana (meditation) section of the Upanishads, we find that various powers or manifestations in nature like the sun, the wind, the sky, the mind, etc. are asked to be meditated upon as Brahman.

Now this sort of meditation is not nature-worship. It becomes so only when the Supreme Being, who is symbolised, is forgotten, and these are worshipped in themselves as such. 'We may worship anything by seeing God *in* it, if we can forget the idol and see God there. We must not project any image upon God. But we may fill any image with that Life which is God. ... He is everything. We may worship a picture as God, but not God as the picture. God in the picture is right, but the picture as God is wrong.'

Thus an object of worship becomes a mere *pratika* in the sense of an idol when the divine is forgotten and the object is worshipped as such but it becomes a *pratika* as devotional substitute or symbol when the divine within is remembered and worshipped through the symbol. The highest symbols of God are the divine incarnations. According to some philosophers they are not to be looked upon as *pratikas* but as God Himself. Objects of worship seem to fall into three categories—symbols including rituals, names of' God and God-men.

23.3 WHY WORSHIP OF *PRATIKAS* IS UNAVOIDABLE

The question may be raised 'Why bother with these symbols at all? Why should we not worship God directly?' Man cannot do this directly without taking the help of concrete aids, some *pratikas*, even as children cannot learn without concrete aids first. Even Christians, Jews and Muslims who disclaim 'idol worship' have all got their own external or mental images, which form for them concrete aids in thinking of, and praying to, the divine. 'When men hear of something very high and wonderful, they all think they will get that, and never stop for a moment to consider that they will have to work their way up to it; they all want to jump there. ... You cannot take a man with a pitchfork and push him up there; we all have to work up gradually.'

All our knowledge, including our knowledge of the external world, is symbolical and indirect. The impression that is made on our brain cells by some 'unknown entity' is projected as our universe on that stimulating 'unknown entity'. Our idea of God is also no exception to this. Anyone who thinks of himself as the body, a material entity, cannot think of himself as he is, that is, as spirit, and is bound to approach God, who is pure spirit, only through symbolic forms, sounds, rituals, etc., which are of a concrete material nature. He is bound to be an 'idolater', a user of *pratikas*, however stoutly he may deny it out of his ignorance.

23.4 *PRATIKA* WORSHIP—PURE AND SIMPLE

Apart from the use of *pratikas* as aids to the worship of the all-pervading Self, there are various forms of *pratika* worship—pure and simple, which may yield results either here or in the hereafter, but have no spiritual significance, that is, cannot be an aid to bhakti and mukti. Among these lower forms of *pratika* worship, the following may be listed: (1) Much of the ritualistic-sacrificial religion of the *Vedas* where gods are invoked by mantras and offerings made to them for the attainment of felicity here and in the heavens hereafter. (2) Ancestor worship in various forms. (3) Worshipping or praying at the tombs of dead ones, dear ones, saints, etc., as done by Christians and Muslims. (4) Spiritism in all forms like séances, invocation and propitiation of spirits, etc. (5) *psychism*, which consists in adoption of measures for attaining super-sensuous power through occult rites and propitiations. (6) Book worship which we find in every religion. It sometimes displaces God Himself. The attitude towards the *Vedas*, the *Koran*, the *Bible*, etc. among fundamentalists of these religions is illustrative of this. Nothing that is not said in the scripture is acceptable to them. When new ideas become prevalent, attempts are made to torture texts by interpretative means and get the meaning they want, so that the new ideas may be incorporated into the accepted tradition by hiding their novelty. When a book becomes an end in itself and more important than God even, then it becomes a true *pratika*.

23.5 THE CHOSEN IDEAL AND THE CONCEPT OF *ISHTA-NISHTHA*

The word *ishta* is derived from the root *ish,* to desire, to choose. *Ishta-nishtha* is the Sanskrit expression for the doctrine of adherence to one's chosen path of spiritual pursuit without any disregard or hatred of those of others. To understand and cultivate this attitude is very important for the development of bhakti. It implies the understanding and acceptance of the following philo- sophical principles:

1. Man's idea of God or Truth varies according to his nature, although God or Truth is one. 'each one of us is an effect, of which our past has been the cause; and as such, there is a peculiar movement, a peculiar train, in each one of us; and therefore each one will have to find way for himself. ... This way, this method, to which each of us is naturally adapted, is called the 'chosen way.'

23.6 PHILOSOPHICAL JUSTIFICATION OF THE PRINCIPLE

This presupposes that men can have different con- ceptions of the same truth or God. There may be a man whose nature is such that he cannot worship a personal God, but can only worship Him as the impersonal, as the highest Self. There will be others who cannot see eye to eye with this idea, but would rather see Him as personal, who could be approached, worshipped and prayed to, expecting responses from Him. The same personal God may be represented in different forms by devotees of various cults and creeds, or He may be worshipped as having no particular form. Even the worshippers of a particular deity may adore Him in differing aspects of His. Thus according to the mental constitution of man, the conception of God can differ. 'There may be millions of radii converging towards the same centre in the sun. The further they are from the centre, the greater is the distance between any two. But as they all meet at the centre, all difference vanishes. There is such a centre, which is the absolute goal of mankind. It is God. We are the radii. The distances between the radii are the constitutional limitations through which alone we can catch the vision of God. While standing on this plane, we are bound each one of us to have a different view of the Absolute Reality; and as such, all views are true, and no one of us need quarrel with another. The only solution lies in approaching the centre. If we try to settle our differences by argument or quarrelling, we shall find that we can go on for hundreds of years'

23.7 OTHER IMPLICATIONS

3. All religious sects, with a traditional background of a line of saintly aspirants and thinkers behind them, are valid paths leading to God. Thus he must know 'that all the various sects of the various religions are the various manifestations of the glory of the same Lord.'

4. A devotee must thus possess an extensive sympathy and power of appreciation of all other creeds and religions. But at the same time, he must have the most intensive love of his own way for approach to God.

5. Without this intensity of love for one's chosen path, a religious cosmopolitanism degenerates into a mere politico-social club life. But one who has intense love for one's own religion only, lands himself in a state in which his so-called love comes to be based upon the hatred of all other religions. Thus he becomes a fanatic of the worst type.

6. *Ishta-nishtha* is a way of life in which both width and intensity are harmoniously blended. Bhakti yoga therefore lays on us the imperative command not to hate or deny any one of the various paths that have led man to salvation.

Sri Ramakrishna's parable of the earl oyster is here relevant. 'The pearl-oyster leaves its bed at the bottom of the sea, and comes up to the surface to catch the rain-water when the star Svāti is in the ascendant. It floats about on the surface of the sea with its shell wide open, until it has succeeded in catching a drop of the rain-water, and then it dives deep down to its sea-bed, and there rests until it has succeeded in fashioning a beautiful pearl out of that rain-drop'

The principle of the *ishta-nishtha* is thus beautifully expressed by Tulsidas: 'Take the sweetness of all, sit with all, take the name of all, say yea, yea, but keep your seat firm.'

24

THE METHOD AND THE MEANS

24.1 BASIC DISCIPLINES OF BHAKTI

There are certain basic disciplines which the Acharyas have considered necessary for the development of bhakti. Some of these are as follows:

1. *Viveka* or discrimination. For Ramanuja this includes also discrimination in taking food, *ahara*. Food, *ahara*, is contaminated by its nature, as in the case of garlic etc., and by physical impurities like dirt. From this idea has arisen all the rigorous caste regulations in the matter of food, which have today degenerated into mere fanaticism and superstition. The truth about it is this: *prakriti* consists of sattva, rajas, and tamas. And our bodies also are made of these constituents. Food is what makes our body. It has to become more and more sattvika if it is to be the medium, for bhakti to manifest. The food materials we take in, form one of the important factors in this kind of purification. The purer the food we take, the better it helps the development of *sattva-suddhi*—the purity of our being. But the present rules of food that some orthodox Hindus pretend to observe

are sheer nonsense. 'but the extravagant, meaningless fanaticism, which has driven religion entirely to the kitchen, as may be noticed in the case of many of our sects, without any hope of the noble truth of that religion ever coming out to the sunlight of spirituality, is a peculiar sort of pure and simple materialism. It is neither Jnāna, nor Bhakti, nor Karma; it is a special kind of lunacy, and those who pin their souls to it are more likely to go to lunatic asylums than to Brahmaloka.'[4]

The rule about *ahara* is given an entirely new meaning by Sankara. ' "That which is gathered in is Ahara." ' So all the sensations we take in and which mould our mind come within the sphere of *ahara*. In this view, *ahara-suddhi* means not merely taking some food superstitiously conceived as pure, but allowing our mind to take in through the senses only ennobling experiences. Both these interpretations have their own validity, when properly understood and applied.

Controlling of the passions, practice of sadhana, sacrificial work, purity, strength and suppression of excessive joy are some of the other factors that help to produce *sattva-suddhi* or purification of being.

---

4   The rules of food given in the past cannot, for one thing, be observed in modern life because of the complexities of life today. Therefore the one practical way the devotee can adopt for purification of food is to offer it to the Lord mentally at least, before he takes his meal—*Publisher.*

24.2 OTHER DISCIPLINES

2. *Vimoka*: it means abandonment of all desires except the one for God. It involves the prevention of *indriyas* (sense organs) from going towards their natural objects. To control and bring them under the guidance of the will is the central virtue in religious culture.

3. *Abhyasa* or practice: It is the effort to make the mind and our organs always directed towards God in place of being engaged in worldly thoughts and occupations. Devotional music is one of the best aids in this.[5]

4. *Kriya*: It means discharge of duties. It involves the five great sacrifices—discharge of man's duties to the gods by worship of them, to sages by study of scriptures, to the manes by offering *tarpana* or prayer for their welfare, to man by works of service and offering of food, to lower creatures by practice of kindness towards them.

5. *Kalyana*: It means purity. It is the bed-rock on which the edifice of bhakti rests. External purity is comparatively easy, but internal purity is very difficult to practise. Ahimsa is one of the essential disciplines to

---

5 The teachers of the devotional school have described *abhyasa* as the nine-limbed devotional discipline, the nine aids being: Hearing of God (*sravanam*), hymns on Him (*kirtanam*), contemplation and remembrance of Him (*smaranam*), service of the world as His feet (*padasevanam*), worship (*archanam*), obeisance (*vandanam*), servantship (*dasyam*), intimacy (*sakhyam*) and self-surrender (*atma-nivedanam*).

attain purity. It means the duty of non-injury to all
beings. In modern Hinduism vegetarianism has become
the essence of ahimsa. Every virtue is abused by man.
There are ascetics of certain sects who will not bother if
their body begins to stink, lest in bathing they should
kill some creatures. There are people who protect cats
and dogs and feed ants as a part of their practice of
ahimsa, but injure their brother men in horrible ways
like exacting ruinous interests, etc. Absence of jealousy
is the sign of a man who practises real ahimsa. Vegetarianism is only the superficial aspect of it. Even the so-
called great men are prone to jealousy. Other aspects of
the practice of purity as enumerated by Ramanuja are:
satya (truthfulness), *arjava* (sincerity), *daya* (doing good
to others without expectation of any return), *anabhidhya*
(not coveting other's wealth and not indulging in vain
brooding over injuries received, or in vain thoughts
and words).

6. *Anavasada* or Strength (lit. not desponding) is another of the great virtues that help the development bhakti.
' "This Atman is not to be attained by the weak", says
the Sruti.' Both physical and mental strength are included in this. Unless there is physical strength and
nervous stamina, 'the shock of reaction resulting from
the attempt to control the organs' cannot be faced.
Weak persons taking to strenuous practice end by developing some incurable malady or eccentricities of

the mind. Cheerfulness of mind is a part of mental strength. But at the same time excessive mirth (*anud-dharsha*) should be avoided. 'Excessive hilarity is quite as objectionable as too much of sad seriousness, and all religious realisation is possible only when the mind is in a steady, peaceful condition of harmonious equilibrium.'

PART 3: BHAKTI YOGA

Section 2: Para Bhakti or Supreme Devotion

25

RENUNCIATION

25.1 PREPARATORY RENUNCIATION

What has been stated till now is about preparatory bhakti, which gradually helps one to attain the state of *para-bhakti* or supreme devotion. Repetition of names, rituals, forms, symbols, etc., forming part of preparatory discipline, are for the purification of the soul. But of all purifiers, renunciation is the most important, and no one can attain *para-bhakti* without that. And what is renunciation? 'When the human soul draws back from the things of the world and tries to go into deeper things; when man, the spirit which has here somehow become concretised and materialised, understands that he is thereby going to be destroyed and to be reduced almost into mere matter, and turns his face away from matter—then begins renunciation, then begins real spiritual growth.'

There are two views of man: One is that man is a body and has a soul; the other is man is a soul and has a body. Worldliness is the consequence of the first, and renunciation of the second. To one who holds the first

view, even faith in God is only a means to obtain worldly
enjoyments here and in a sensual heaven hereafter. They
are like swine, wallowing in the mire of the senses, un-
able to see anything beyond. Though physically they are
men, spiritually they are stagnating at the animal level,
living as they do exclusively for sensuous satisfaction.
'Slaves of this world, slaves of the senses, let us rouse
ourselves; there is something higher than this sense-life.
Do you think that man, the Infinite Spirit was born to
be a slave to his eyes, his nose, and his ears? There is an
Infinite, Omniscient Spirit behind that can do everything, break every bond; and that Spirit we are, and we
get that power through love.'

So long as our needs are confined within the narrow
limits of this physical universe, we will not feel any need
for God. Bhakti proceeds out of a real want. Ordinarily
man wants only food, clothing, wealth, sex satisfaction,
acquisition of power, fulfilment of ambitions, etc. When
all these lower desires drop off little by little, man will
begin to want God in a real sense. Until this purification through renunciation is effected, man's religion
is clouded heavily by materialistic demand, and there
is very little difference between a devotee of this type
and a materialist who lives honestly without any faith
in God and higher life.

Renunciation is involved in all the *yogas*—in karma
yoga as giving up all fruits of action, in raja yoga by

recognition of the eternal separation of the Soul from nature, and in *jnana yoga* by recognising at the start itself that this solid-looking nature is all an appearance.

25.2 THE SPECIAL FEATURE OF THE BHAKTA'S RENUNCIATION

But the bhakta's renunciation differs from all these because of its effortless naturalness. It is natural for man to give up a previous object of love when something new and more attractive begins to draw his mind. There is no forcible effort here to drive off from the mind the previous object of love; it is naturally ejected by the new love because the mind finds the new love more delightful than the old one. The more primitive and sensuous the mind, the more is it centred in the body and its pleasures. 'No man can enjoy a meal with the same gusto or pleasure as a dog or a wolf, but those pleasures which a man gets from intellectual experiences and achievements, the dog can never enjoy. At first, pleasure is in association with the lowest senses; but as soon as an animal reaches a higher plane of existence, the lower kind of pleasures becomes less intense. In human society, the nearer the man is to the animal, the stronger is his pleasure in the senses; and the higher and the more cultured the man is, the greater is his pleasure in intellectual and such other finer pursuits. So when a man

gets even higher than the plane of the intellect, higher
than that of mere thought, when he gets to the plane
of spirituality and of divine inspiration, he finds there
a state of bliss, compared with which all the pleasures
of the senses, or even of the intellect, are as nothing.
When the moon shines brightly, all the stars become
dim; and when the sun shines, the moon herself becomes dim.' The renunciation of the bhakta is comparable to these evolutions. It comes naturally. When the
Lord becomes attractive, the attachments for worldly
objects naturally fall off. Not only that, even all external forms, considered so essential by people ordinarily,
fall off, as devotion develops into *para-bhakti*, that is, as
devotion takes on its higher forms of expression. 'Forms
vanish, rituals fly away, books are superseded; images,
temples, churches, religions and sects, countries and
nationalities—all these little limitations and bondages
fall off by their own nature from him who knows this
love of God. Nothing remains to bind him or fetter his
freedom. A ship, all of a sudden, comes near a mag-
netic rock, and its iron bolts and bars are all attracted
and drawn out, and the planks get loosened and freely
float on the water. Divine grace thus loosens the bind-
ing bolts and bars of the soul, and it becomes free. So
in this renunciation auxiliary to devotion, there is no
harshness, no dryness no struggle, nor repression nor
suppression. The Bhakta has not to suppress any single

one of his emotions, he only strives to intensify them and direct them to God.'

25.3 THE BHAKTA'S RENUNCIATION RESULTS FROM LOVE

It is the same feeling of love, well or ill-directed, that impels one man to do good and to give all he has to the poor, while it makes another man cut the throats of his brethren and take away all their possessions. It is the same emotion that gives us the pure and holy conjugal love between husband and wife, as well as that sort of love which goes to satisfy the lowest forms of animal passion.'love, the intense longing for association, the strong desire on the part of two to become one—and it may be, after all, of all to become merged in one—is being manifested everywhere in higher or lower forms as the case may be.

Bhakti-Yoga is the science of higher love. It shows us how to direct it; it shows us how to control it, how to manage it, how to use it, how to give it a new aim, as it were, and from it obtain the highest and most glorious results, that is, how to make it lead us to spiritual blessedness. Bhakti-Yoga does not say, "Give up"; it only says, "Love; love the Highest!"—and everything low naturally falls off from him, the object of whose love is the Highest.'

What is required in this yoga is that our quest after the beautiful should be directed towards God. The beauty in the human face, in the sky, in the star, in the moon—is only the partial apprehension of the real all-embracing divine beauty. 'Do not look upon humanity as the centre of all your human and higher interests. Stand as a witness, as a student, and observe the phenomena of nature. Have the feeling of personal non-attachment with regard to man, and see how this mighty feeling of love is working itself out in the world. Sometimes a little friction is produced, but that is only in the course of the struggle to attain the higher real love. Sometimes there is a little fight or a little fall; but it is all only by the way. Stand aside, and freely let these frictions come. You feel the frictions only when you are in the current of the world, but when you are outside of it simply as a witness and as a student, you will be able to see that there are millions and millions of channels in which God is manifesting Himself as Love.'

25.4 GOD AS THE CENTRE OF ATTRACTION (HARI)

One of the names of the Lord in Sanskrit is Hari, and means 'He attracts all things to Himself.' Even the lowest forms of attraction derive their power from God Himself. The worldly attraction of wife, child, friends, etc., is the same as the attraction of the divine, but ignorantly felt. The Lord is the great magnet, and we are like iron filings constantly attracted by Him. All the struggles in life are intended to make man go to Him ultimately and be one with Him.

A follower of bhakti yoga understands this, and wants to avoid the outer forms of this attraction and go to Him who is the centre of it. 'That is to say, the Bhakta's renunciation is that Vairāgya or non-attachment for all things that are not God which results from Anurāga or great attachment to God. ... Then it is that we begin to understand what Para-Bhakti is.' Such a person endowed with *para-bhakti* rises above all forms and symbols. He alone is able to love man without motive or practise the brotherhood of man. He does not see man as man but beholds his beloved everywhere. Such devotees never react in the spirit of jealousy or hatred, as they realise the presence of the divine everywhere and in everything through love.

25.5 NATURALNESS OF BHAKTI YOGA

The *Bhagavad Gita* maintains that the path of the Absolute, i.e., the path of knowledge, is difficult for embodied beings, that is, for men in whom the body consciousness is too strong. But the way is far easier for those who worship God as personal and offer all their actions to Him and live in entire reliance on Him.

This has to be remembered by all aspirants. There is a tendency to assume oneself to be very clever and pretend to love or follow the path of knowledge, forgetting that no one who considers the care-taking of the body as the end-all of life can succeed in it. 'The devil can and indeed does cite the scriptures for his own purpose; and thus the way of knowledge appears to offer justification to what the bad man does, as much as it offers inducements to what the good man does. This is the great danger in Jnana-Yoga. But Bhakti-Yoga is natural, sweet, and gentle; the Bhakta does not take such high flights as the Jnana-Yogi, and, therefore, he is not apt to have such big falls.'

According to the bhakti discipline, the emotions of the human heart are not wrong in themselves. Only they have to be controlled and directed to God. Through communing with Him in any way, through any of the passions and emotions of the heart, the aspirant gets purified.

26

STAGES OF BHAKTI

The following are some of the expressions of true devotion:

1. *Sraddha* or Reverence: This is the beginning of all devotion, and it is the first shoot of love. Places of worship and teachers of religion are revered, because they are connected with God. Disciplinary devotion is based on reverence.

2. *Priti*: This is the state when man takes pleasure in God. Practice of devotional disciplines then becomes a matter of joy.

3. *Viraha*: It is the longing of the soul for being in the presence of the Lord and the anguish it experiences when it could not be. It is a state of mind which is painful but yet sweet. Everything other than God becomes insipid and positively obnoxious to one who is possessed of this state.

4. *Tadartha-prana-sandhana*: It is a state in which life itself is maintained for the sake of the Lord, and it is

considered beautiful and worth living only on account of the love of Him. Without Him life will not remain even for a moment.

5. *Tadiyata*: It means '*His-ness*' or belonging to Him'. This is the nature of the devotee transformed by the divine touch. All his purposes in life are fulfilled, and he is fully established in the experience of 'belonging to God.' Of them it is said in the *Bhagavata*: 'O king, such is the blessed quality of Hari that even those who have become satisfied with everything, all the knots of whose hearts have been cut asunder, even they love the Lord for love's sake.... When a man has forgotten himself altogether, and does not feel that anything belongs to him, then he acquires the state of "Tadiyata"; everything is sacred to him, because it belongs to the Beloved.'

26.2 UNIVERSAL LOVE AND HOW IT LEADS TO SELF-SURRENDER

Universal love becomes possible only through love of God. We may love individuals or groups, but it will not take us anywhere near what is called universal love. It is only when we arrive at the highest generalisation that we cover all the individuals that come under it. God is the *samashti*, the generalised universal whole, and all things in the universe are His parts, differentiated and made manifest. If we love that sum total, we love everything. Thus the power to love all comes only to one who loves God first; for God-love destroys the love for our little self and our body, which is the factor that stands in the way of the development of universal love.

In the eyes of such a devotee everything belongs to Him; all are His children, His body, His manifestation. He loses all sense of fear; pleasure and pain become alike to him. 'Knowing that Hari, the Lord, is in every being, the wise have thus to manifest unswerving love towards all beings.'

He develops also perfect self-surrender and the conviction that nothing that happens is against him (*apratikulyata*). 'the Bhakta declares that we have to hold ourselves as if we are altogether dead to all the things of the world; and that is indeed self-surrender. Let things come as they may. This is the meaning of "Thy will be done"—not going about fighting and struggling and thinking all the while that God wills all our own weaknesses and worldly ambitions.' The perfected bhakta's idea must be never to will and work for himself. ' "Lord, they build high temples in Your name; they make large gifts in Your name; I am poor; I have nothing; so I take this body of mine and place it at Your feet. Do not give me up, O Lord". ... The peace of the Bhakta's calm resignation is a peace that passeth all understanding ... His Apratikulya is a state of the mind in which it has no interests and naturally knows nothing that is opposed to it.' All attachments fall away. The attachment of love of God effectively breaks all other bondages.

27

THE PEAK OF BHAKTI

27.1 THE HIGHER KNOWLEDGE AND THE HIGHER LOVE ARE ONE TO THE TRUE LOVER

The Upanishads make a distinction between two forms of knowledge—*para* (the higher one relating to God) and *apara* (relating to secular subjects).

So also in bhakti there is para-bhakti, the supreme love, and apara-bhakti, the lower discipline which gradually leads to this higher attainment. Para-Bhakti has been defined in Devi-Bhagavata: ' "As oil poured from one vessel to another falls in an unbroken line, so, when the mind in an unbroken stream thinks of the Lord, we have what is called Para-Bhakti or supreme love" ' The devotee becomes capable of adoring the lord in his own heart, without the help of any forms, symbols, books or dogmas. All other forms of devotion are preparatory to this state, and are not ends in themselves. When such love is generated, the bhakta thinks of God alone in all circumstances, favourable or unfavourable.

Such a high expression of love manifests only when

all thoughts of returns are eliminated from the mind. Ordinarily love is seen to flourish only when it is returned or when some reward is expected. In para-bhakti man loves God for the sake of love, and continues to love Him irrespective of any response from Him. Between such higher love (*para-bhakti*) and higher knowledge (*jnana*), there is no difference.

27.2 THE TRIANGLE OF LOVE

Bhakti (love) may be compared to a triangle, the three angles or sides of it representing the characteristics of true love.

The first feature is that love knows no bargaining. So long as man's approach to God is motivated by favours to be derived from Him, there can be no true love. The true bhakta loves Him because He is lovable and expects no return. Begging is not the language of love. Even worshipping Him for the sake of salvation is inferior to this highest ideal of love.

The second feature of the triangle of love is that it knows no fear. Low types of men only worship a God who has a whip in one hand and a sceptre in the other, the idea being that punishment will follow if he is disobeyed. 'Fear comes from the selfish idea of cutting one's self off from the universe. The smaller and the more selfish I make myself, the more is my fear. If a man thinks

he is a little nothing, fear will surely come upon him.
And the less you think of yourself as an insignificant
person, the less fear there will be for you.6 So long as
there is the least spark of fear in you there can be no
love there. Love and fear are incompatible; God is never
to be feared by those who love Him.'

'The third angle of the love-triangle is that love
knows no rival, for in it is always embodied the lover's
highest ideal. ... The synthesis of all the highest ideals
of beauty, of sublimity, and of power gives us the com-
pletest conception of the loving and lovable God.' If
you take a philosophical view of worship, we find each
man projecting his own ideal and worshipping it. 'This
external world is only the world of suggestion. All that
we see, we see project out of our own minds. A grain
of sand gets washed into the shell of an oyster and irri-
tates it. The irritation produces a secretion in the oyster,
which covers the grain of sand and the beautiful pearl
is the result. Similarly, external things furnish us with
suggestions, over which we project our own ideals and
make our objects. The wicked see this world as a perfect
hell, and the good as a perfect heaven. Lovers see this
world as full of love, and haters as full of hatred; fight-
ers see nothing but strife, and the peaceful as nothing

6   This means that the more you think you are a spirit and not
a perishable body, the more you will be free from fear. It should
not be understood as a call to be a bloated egotist—Publisher.

but peace. The perfect man sees nothing but God. So we always worship our highest ideal, and when we have reached the point, where we love the ideal as the ideal, all arguments and doubts vanish forever. Who cares whether God can be demonstrated or not? The ideal can never go, because it is a part of my own nature. I shall only question the ideal when I question my own existence, and as I cannot question the one, I cannot question the other.' But according to the mental development of man, he at first projects imperfect conceptions of this ideal and worships it. When he realises the imperfection of all such projections, he never tries to project it but worships the ideal itself as ideal, from the highest standpoint of love.

27.3 GOD OF LOVE IS HIS OWN PROOF

When proof for the existence of God is asked, people mostly have in mind a creator God or a magistrate God, but not a God of love who is self-evident for the devotee of the highest order. Having failed to project the highest ideal of perfection in external objects, he 'acquires the power of realising the highest and the most generalised abstract ideal entirely as an abstraction that is to him quite alive and real. ... It requires no proofs to demonstrate the existence of the beloved to the lover.'

When one thinks of oneself as comprehended in the

universal, there can be no selfishness in one. But when by mistake one thinks of oneself as a little something, love becomes particularised and narrowed. But this whole, the universal, is the God of the bhakta, and as all parts are included in the whole, his love too takes a universal turn. He has no need of temples and churches, although he may respect them. 'He finds Him in the temple as well as out of the temple, he finds Him in the saint's saintliness as well as in the wicked man's wickedness, because he has Him already seated in glory in his own heart as the one Almighty inextinguishable Light of Love which is ever shining and eternally present.'

27.4 HUMAN REPRESENTATION OF THE DIVINE IDEAL OF LOVE

The teachers of the doctrine of bhakti have tried to represent this inexpressible divine love in terms of human love and its varied forms. Any expression of the Infinite in terms of the finite has its imperfection. But that is unavoidable, it being the only means possible. 'The whole universe is to us a writing of the Infinite in the language of the finite.' These forms of love are graded as follows according to the intensity of the personal affection involved,

1. *Santa:* Devotion that has risen above ceremonial-

ism and is constant and philosophically oriented but is without that madness of intensely active love, is called *santa*. Such bhakti is calm, peaceful and gentle.

2. *Dasya or servantship:* This comes when the devotee develops the feeling that he is a faithful and eternal servant of God and has attachment to Him appropriate to this relationship.

3. *Sakhya or friendship:* A sense of equality with the Lord, confidence, and a lack of awe in the face of His divine majesties are characteristic of this form of love. More over the devotee becomes a playmate of God in His grand cosmic sport. The doctrine of the universe as the divine *lila* or sport is as follows: God, the perfect being, has no wants, and hence no purpose yet to be achieved can be attributed to His creative activity. So it has to be described as His sport, and the devotee must feel that he is a participant in this divine sport. He is to feel that God is his eternal playmate, and His creation, a sport. 'as soon as you give up the serious idea of reality as the characteristic of the changing incidents of the three minutes of life and know it to be but a stage on which we are playing, helping Him to play, at once misery ceases for you. ... He is playing when He is building up earths, and suns, and moons; He is playing with the human heart, with animals, with plants. We are His chessmen. ... and we are consciously or unconsciously helping in His play. And, oh, bliss! we are His playmates!'

4. *Vatsalya:* It means loving God as our child. Here the fear-creating majesty of God is completely forgotten. Also reverence, obedience and such restraining influences are abandoned. God becomes a little child needing the devotee's love and protection. Such a form of love is possible only in societies that accept the idea of divine incarnation.

5. *Madhura or conjugal:* In devotional philosophy, this is considered the highest and the most intense form of devotion. The love between a man and a woman, which is the most powerful form of human love, is utilised in the cultivation of devotion. God is the only male and the souls are his wives, and the devotee develops a passionate love for Him in the light of this relationship. 'All loves and all passions of the human heart must go to God. He is the Beloved. Whom else can this heart love? ... Who in this universe is more fit to become the husband than He?'

Often devotees cultivating this form of love utilise the language and form of human love in their descriptions of these diverse sentiments. Those who look at these descriptions from a purely physical point of view misunderstand it; for, only when the dominance of the physical sense has abated, can this form of love be practised or understood. 'Fools do not understand this; they never will. They look at it only with the physical eye. They do not understand the mad throes of this spiritual love. How can they? "For one kiss of Thy lips, O Beloved! One who has been kissed by Thee, has his thirst for Thee increasing for ever, all his sorrows vanish, and he forgets all things except Thee alone." Aspire after that kiss of the Beloved, that touch of His lips which makes the Bhakta mad, which makes of man a god. To him, who has been blessed with such a kiss, the whole of nature changes, worlds vanish, suns and moons die out, and the universe itself melts away into that one infinite ocean of love. That is the perfection of the madness of love.'

To further intensify the sense of attachment to, and dependence on God, bhaktas take up the symbolism of the illicit love of a girl for her lover. The highest illustration of this we get in the love of the *Gopis* for Krishna. 'Human language cannot describe how Krishna in the groves of Vrindā was madly loved, how at the sound of his voice the ever-blessed Gopis rushed out to meet him, forgetting everything, forgetting this world and its ties, its duties, its joys, and its sorrows. Man, O man, you speak of divine love and at the same time are able to attend to all the vanities of this world—are you sincere? " Where Rāma is, there is no room for any desire—where desire is, there is no room for Rama; these never coexist—like light and darkness they are never together." '

This type of *prema bhakti*, intense love of God, sets at naught all worldly values. To a critic of such intense

God-love, Sri Ramakrishna once replied: ' "My friends, the whole world is a lunatic asylum. Some are mad after worldly love, some after name, some after fame, some after money, some after salvation and going to heaven. In this big lunatic asylum I am also mad, I am mad after God. If you are mad after money, I am mad after God. You are mad; so am I. I think my madness is after all the best.'

'We all have to begin as dualists in the religion of love. God is to us a separate Being, and we feel ourselves to be separate beings also. Love then comes in the middle, and man begins to approach God, and God also comes nearer and nearer to man. Man takes up all the various relationships of life, as father, as mother, as son, as friend, as master, as lover, and projects them on his ideal of love, on his God. To him God exists as all these, and the last point of his progress is reached when he feels that he has become absolutely merged in the object of his worship.'

28

THE GIST OF BHAKTI YOGA

Bhakti in its highest sense means spontaneous and continuous attraction of the mind to God under all circumstances, favourable and unfavourable. It implies a sense of supreme delight in Him and the knowledge that He is the highest of all beings. It is not motivated by any thought of return, but finds its fulfilment in the loving service of Him.

In its wider connotation bhakti includes also all the disciplines leading gradually to this attainment. To distinguish these preparatory disciplines from this highest attainment, they are described as *gauni bhakti* (devotion based on external aids), while the latter is called *para* or *prema bhakti* (spontaneous loving devotion).

While most of the devotees do not concern themselves with philosophy, it is better to have an understanding of the most important concepts concerned with devotional thought. The first and most important of these is that of God. He is described as the source and support of all manifested phenomena and life. He is also described in His essence as inexpressible Love.

Is He then different from Brahman, the impersonal Absolute of the Vedanta? He is not. Brahman is both personal and impersonal. When one is conscious of one's individuality and practises a devotional attitude towards the Supreme Being, Brahman presents Himself as the personal God or *Iswara*. He is the Absolute Himself, and not a being different from Him or inferior to Him. A distinction is made only because bhakti or devotion can be practised only in relation to a personal being.

The first thing for a person entering seriously on the path of devotion is to be under the direction of a genuine guru or spiritual teacher. A genuine guru is one who lives a holy life, observes the spirit of the scriptures, who has no selfish motives in accepting disciples, and who is moved only by love. And a true disciple is one who is dissatisfied with the pursuit of worldly values, who has a longing of God, who is full of faith and sincerity, and who is full of earnestness to follow the instructions given to him.

Besides giving general instructions, the teacher transmits to the disciple a sacred mantra, a word symbol, by repeating and meditating on which with devotion the spiritual power in the disciple gets roused up in course of time. The most universal of all these sound-symbols is Om. Om is the basic sound out of which all other sounds have come out, and so it represents the universal and all-embracing being in His manifestation as the All. So Om is taken as the one correct syllable to represent the Universal Being, Brahman. Various aspects of the Supreme Being are apprehended by different people according to the dominant *tattva* (element) in them, and there are mantras representing these different aspects. All these mantras representing different aspects of the Supreme Being have been discovered by great sages in their deepest meditation.

Besides sound symbols or names of God in His various aspects, symbols enter very largely into the devotional disciplines applicable to man in the early stages of spiritual development. Rituals, images, mantras, sacred designs, divine forms, God-men, impressive natural phenomena like the sun, the air, sky, etc.—all these are the various symbols used for helping man towards the contemplation of the Universal Being, *Iswara*. They are called *pratikas*. When the devotee seeks to worship the Supreme Being with their help, such worship is included in bhakti discipline. But it becomes mere *pratika* worship in the sense of idolatory when the worshipper, without seeing Brahman through them, seeks to worship and propitiate them in themselves for various selfish gains. While such forms of *pratika* worship may bring fruits in this world and the next as in the case of many of the ritualistic karmas of the *Vedas* and *Tantras*, they cannot bring bhakti and mukti. Only the worship of the Supreme Being, *Iswara*, can give bhakti and mukti.

The worship of the personalised forms of God like Siva, Vishnu and the Devi, who are identified with the godhead in their respective cult theologies, may also be considered to be *pratika* worship by a philosophical mind. But the identification of these conceptions with godhead in the minds of their devotees is so close and inborn, that they will say they are the very godhead and not mere symbols representing Him. The incarnations are other divine manifestations which transcend the limits of symbolism and are looked upon as identical with Godhead. These deities and incarnations are worshipped through symbols called *pratimas* or images. The philosophy of *pratikas* is applicable to the *pratimas* also. However, in devotional schools, the sense of real presence of the divine in the image is so intense that the image itself is treated with worshipful reverence as the very divine. Such worship should be distinguished from idolatry or worship of beings other than God. Worship of divine images in the sense described above is a part of the devotional discipline.

Worship of *pratikas* is an absolute necessity for the spiritual development of man, and it enters into the forms of prayer and divine service even of sects that stoutly oppose it. Their opposition to symbols means only opposition to others' symbols and not the abandonment of them totally. Intellectuals may use high sounding words to describe the divine as omnipotent, omniscient, all-pervading, etc., but these mean nothing beyond their spelling except when these are identified with or viewed through some concrete objects, physical or mental, which the human mind can grasp. As long as we are centred in body consciousness, we cannot conceive of God as pure spirit and we have necessarily got to approach Him through symbols and forms.

There are certain qualities of mind which an aspirant has necessarily got to cultivate. These are as follows: 1. *Viveka:* It is the capacity to select what is spiritually ennobling and reject the degrading ones. It means also *ahara-suddhi* or taking in only purifying food and elevating sense impressions. 2. *Vimoka:* It signifies the abandonment of all desires except the one for God and the consequent withholding of the mind and senses from running after sensuous satisfactions. The cultivation of bhakti thus requires the abandonment of attachment for worldly objects (*vairagya*). But it is cultivated naturally and gradually. As love of God increases, attraction for other things disappears. And conversely, only with perfect non-attachment would true bhakti develop. 3. *Kriya:* It means the discharge of one's duties in the spirit of an offering to God and the performance of the *pancha-maha-yajnas*, the five kinds of sacrifices required of men. 4. *Abhyasa:* It is the practice of the specific devotional disciplines, by means of which the mind is fixed on God.

The practice of *vava-vidha bhakti* (nine-fold devotional
discipline) comes under this. 5. *Kalyana:* It means purity in body and mind. The essence of mental purify is
practice of ahimsa. Ahimsa is not mere non-killing in
a physical sense, but abandonment of jealousy, which
is one of the most befouling influences on character-
traits. The practice of *brahmacharya* (continence), *asteya*
(non-exploitation), *satya* (truth), and *aparigraha* (non-
avariciousness) come within it.

By long practice of preparatory disciplines, the aspirant develops *para-bhakti*, the supreme unmotivated
love of God as the Universal Being. The development
takes place through the following stages: (1) *Sraddha* or
faith leading to the earnest practice of devotional disciplines, (2) *Priti* or joy in the contemplation of God,
(3) *Viraha* or intense and anxious yearning for Him.
(4) *Tadartha-prana-sandhana*, which means living only
for His sake and therefore having no other interest except He. (5) *Tadiyata* or the state when man forgets his
little self and becomes entirely centred in Him. It is the
state of perfect self-surrender which gives 'peace that
passeth all understanding'.

Para-bhakti has three important features, which may
be termed as the three angles of the triangle of love.
These are: (1) Love seeks no return, for it is the nature of
pure Love to give and not to take or demand. (2) Love
knows no fear: for, they are incompatible. Fear is the

result of narrow self-centredness based on the body and its welfare. In true love the devotee surrenders himself completely to Him and feels himself to be a part and parcel of Him. There is no place for fear in such a state of mind. (3) Love knows no rival; for, in it is embodied the devotee's highest ideal. After projecting this ideal on external objects and meeting with repeated disappointments, the devotee learns to love the highest ideal in itself. It becomes to him a living, palpable reality, which includes in itself all that exists. No narrow love draws him anymore. In the love of the all-inclusive being, everything is included, and the bhakta attains to universal love. He no longer requires symbols or temples for worship. Love becomes spontaneous, requiring no external aid. The bhakta sees God in everything and that is his worship.

In the discipline of bhakti, the practice of renunciation consists not in destroying any of man's affections, but in giving them a godward turn. So the teachers of bhakti have taught how to channelise human affections into forms of God-love known as the *bhavas*. These *bhavas* are classified as follows:

(1) *Santa* or placid and philosophical without much of personal element in it. (2) *Dasya* or attitude of a servant, (3) *Apatya* or attitude of a son to a father (4) *Sakhya* or relation of a friend towards a friend, (5) *Vatsalya* or the affection of a parent towards a child and (6) *Madhura*

or sweet, which can take the form of pure conjugal love or of illegitimate love between a lover and a sweet-heart.

In the highest state of *para-bhakti* the lover loses himself in the beloved and attains to the state of non-duality. Thus the highest form of knowledge and the highest form of bhakti are one and the same in the end, though at the disciplinary stage they may differ. Love and knowledge are thus the obverse and the reverse of the same coin even as personal *Iswara* and impersonal Brahman are.

PART 4: JNANA YOGA

29

THE NEED FOR RELIGION

29.1 THE ORIGIN OF RELIGIONS: ANCESTOR WORSHIP AND NATURE WORSHIP

Of all the forces working for moulding the destinies of the human race, religion has been the most potent and all-pervasive influence. Its bond has often proved stronger in holding men together than even race, language, climate, descent and other factors.

There are two main theories among anthropologists about the origin of religion. Some hold that it had its origin in ancestor worship, as typified by the social history of Egypt, Babylonia and China. The Egyptians had the idea of a double in the human body, which could be helped on to live if the dead body were preserved intact. So they built the pyramids to keep embalmed the dead bodies of kings and other worthies. The Babylonians also had the idea of the double, but they conceived of the double as terrorising the living if it is not given food and drink. In China, ancestor-worship is the prevailing religion even now.

The other idea is that religion originated from nature-worship. The religion of the ancient Aryans is an
instance in point. The great powers of nature are person-
ified into Gods. This tendency is found also among the
Greeks, the ancient Germans and the Scandinavians.

Though these two theories seem to be different, they
have their origin in man's struggle to transcend the
limitations of the senses. He has a strong feeling that
the sense life does not exhaust his whole being. He got
a clue to this perhaps from the mysterious, everyday
experience of dream in which the mental life of man
seems to be separated from the body.

29.2 INSPIRATION AS THE SOURCE OF RELIGION

Side by side, man was discovering a higher state of
mind than waking and dreaming, in the experience of
ecstasy, which gave him the idea of inspiration as the
source of his religious convictions. The founders of all
religions claim to have had experience of such a state,
in which they came face to face with facts relating to
the spiritual kingdom with an intensity of awareness
greater than that of normal experience. Thus the rishis
from whom the *Vedas* have come, did not write the *Vedas*,
but saw and experienced the thought expressed in their
hymns. 'Even Buddhism, which does not accept a God
or soul, accepts this idea of inspiration; for, the Bud-

dha did not reason out the existence of the moral law, but discovered it in the super-sensuous state attained through meditation.' Thus all religions accept the idea that at certain moments the mind can transcend sense perception and reason, and come to know the spiritual verities directly.

29.3 RELIGION AS THE BASIS OF ETHICS: FUTILITY OF UTILITARIANISM

The one fact that stands out in all the different religions is that there is an ideal unit abstraction, which is placed before us, either in the form of a personal, or an Impersonal Being, or a Presence, or the moral law. Even the humblest man has this ideal of infinite power and other excellences. He tries to realise this Infinite in physical terms, but finds he cannot do it. Then he renounces this attempt in favour of super-sensuous methods. Thus renunciation is the basis of all ethics.

Ethics is based upon the idea 'Not I, but thou.' On the other hand, the senses say 'Myself first.' Perfect self-abnegation is the ideal of ethics. It means the abandonment of individuality. Generally men are afraid to be told that they have to give up their individuality, and yet speak of high ethical ideals, without realising that these are not compatible with clinging to individuality.

Utilitarian standards cannot give a satisfactory

basis for ethics. Why should I care for the happiness of the largest number, if I can make myself more happy through methods that will make others unhappy? Utilitarianism has no answer for this. Secondly, social utility is too narrow a concept. Possibly it is a passing stage through which we are going to a higher evolution where utility has no application. But a morality based on spiritual perception has the whole of infinite man for its scope. It takes up the individual in his relation to the Infinite—from his primitive state to the stage of his attainment of divinity. It takes up the society too. Just as it applies to the individual and has eternal relations with eternal verities, it must necessarily apply to the whole of society, in whatever condition it may be at any given time. Ethics cannot stand as an end in itself, if it is separated from the super-sensuous sanction in man's experience of an infinite and enduring ideal. This ideal comes first, and ethics only stems from it. Thus there is always the necessity of a spiritual religion for mankind.

As far back as the days of the Chinese sage Confucius, it was said, ' "Let us take care of this world: and then, when we have finished with this world, we will take care of other world.' "

But it is forgotten that if too much attention to the 'spiritual' will affect our practical relations, it is equally true that too much concern with the 'practical' would make us materialistic and slaves of nature.

Man is man so long as he is struggling to rise above nature. Nature, with which he is in confrontation, is both external and internal. The conquest of external nature, which science purports to do, impresses the ordinary run of mankind, who derive pleasure mainly from things external and are impressed by manifestations of physical strength. But there are a few who are thoughtful and introspective and get a glimpse of something higher than matter, of the Infinite that transcends the senses. They are the spiritual type, and they are the mainspring of the strength of every race. The utilitarian may find the greatest pleasure in eating, as a dog too does, or in possessing the maximum, as some others do. The lower the type of humanity, the greater the addiction to the pleasures of the senses. The cultured and the educated ones only feel interest in arts, sciences and philosophy. Spirituality is the highest of all such values, and its pursuit is found only among the most highly evolved. They feel that the quest for the Infinite, the effort to go beyond the limitations of the senses, the struggle involved in it, is itself the grandest and the most glorious of experiences that man can have. The utilitarian cannot ignore this type. For, it is from their ranks that the world-movers, whose spirit works through hundreds and thousands of ages, whose life ignites others with a spiritual fire, have come. Their motive power came from religion. Religion is the greatest

motive power for realising that infinite energy which
is the birthright and nature of every man. In building
up character, in making for everything that is good
and great, in bringing peace to others and peace to
one's own self, religion is the highest motive power and,
therefore, ought to be studied from that standpoint.'

29.5 NEED OF UNIVERSAL OUTLOOK
IN RELIGIOUS MATTERS

Religion in the future has, however, to be studied
from a higher standpoint. Man has to overcome the
deeply established tribal mentality in his conception of
God and religion. A tribal God and religion are just like
a nationalistic state, ready to be imposed by the victor
on the vanquished in the course of material struggle for
domination. Religion then becomes politics, and loses
its ennobling spiritual character. Universality of outlook
consisting in a readiness to accept the other man's way
of thought and of worship has become unavoidable.
The world has become too small, thanks to the modern
ways of communication, and the future religion has to
be universal. It has to be inclusive, and not exclusive,
by abandoning the tendency to look down upon one
another with contempt because of the differences in
the ideals of God they entertain. The ideas of the personal God, the impersonal, the Infinite, the moral law,

the ideal man—all these have to come under the defin-ition of religion. And when religions have become thus broadened, their power for good will have increased a hundredfold. If religions have done harm to the world in the past, it was only on account of the narrowness of those who practised them. In place of that, there should be a fellow-feeling among them, springing from mutual esteem and respect, and not the condescending and pat-ronising attitude unfortunately in vogue now. There is also the need for reconciliation of the claims of religion and science, between the study of nature internal to us and what is called external nature.

A religion so broad-based and universal will have a more tremendous influence than ever in the past. Some think that religions are dying and spiritual ideals are on the wane. On the other hand, the truth is that they have just begun to grow. In the past, religion was in the hands of a few priests, and its practice was confined to temples, ceremonials and profession of dogmas of a narrow type. 'But when we come to the real, spiritual, universal concept, then, and then alone, religion will become real and living; it will come into our very na-ture, live in our every movement, penetrate every pore of our society, and be infinitely more a power for good than it has ever been before.'

MAN'S TRUE NATURE

30.1 PRECEDENCE OF SPIRIT OVER MATTER

Though man clings very tenaciously to the world revealed by the senses and their enjoyment, he is often forced to stop and ask, 'Is this real?' It is death, which in a twinkling of the eye removes everything he held as real and valuable that makes him put this question. So long as death is there as the culmination of man's life here, no materialistic thinker can stifle man's question, 'What is beyond? ... "Is death the end of all these things to which we are clinging, as if they were the most real of all realities, the most substantial of all substances?" What becomes of the energies of the mind? and so on.

Discussing this question, two schools of thought give two opposite answers. The materialist's answer is the theory that thought is only a by-product of physical energies and disappears with the death of the body, leaving nothing of it to survive. But this does not answer the question at issue—namely, how it is that this meaningful and complex combination of particles of matter that we call the body comes into existence. Meaning and design presuppose an intelligence. So this evolution must be directed by an intelligent principle which precedes the body. Hence to say that this intelligent principle is itself a product of the body, is only to put the cart before the horse. The more natural explanation will be that the same force that functions in the body now has been there already to draw particles from its environment and fashion the body. Even scientifically speaking, matter is only a state of energy and does not exist independent of it. So from the most ancient times, human thought has held that there is behind the external body, a spiritual body that survives the physical body and attains to higher evolution.

30.2 ENQUIRY INTO THE
SPIRITUAL NATURE OF MAN

Side by side there was also the idea that the present man is a degeneration of a more perfect state of existence. The Hindus have the idea that there was the perfect age of *satya yuga* in which man was without any defect or evil and lived a divine life, from which he has degenerated into what he is in later ages. The *Bible* too has the myth of Adam and Eve. Now those myths are not mere cock and bull stories, but expressions of certain deep philosophical thoughts through a peculiar kind of symbolic stories. It means that in what you call 'man', with all his limitations, perfection, which is the same as the divine, is present in an involved state, and that evolution is only the effort towards the restoration of this divine nature into its full manifestation.

It is in this idea of the latent divinity of man that we should seek the reconciliation of the modern doctrine of man as a product of natural evolution, with the ancient idea of his being a spirit transcending this body. Evolution is inconceivable without an involution, as science cannot conceive of getting from any machine energy over and above what has already been put into it in another form. So if a perfect man is an evolute from a mollusc, then that perfect man must be accepted as being already involved in the mollusc. So, the enquiry about this spiritual energy in man, which transcends the body, which in fact selects particles of matter to form bodies from the lowest to the highest scale of evolution, has its relevancy, and has to be accepted. Without it, man's quest after knowledge about himself and nature will not be complete.

At first man conceived of this spiritual force as a bright body within the physical body. But if it is body, it must be a combination of parts like the physical body itself, and must therefore be perishable. So that idea was given up by philosophic thinkers, and just like the physical body itself, the bright body that survives, was also conceived as a field for the spirit, the Atman, to work with or manifest. Even mind is only its instrument. Discussions about the nature of the spirit, which is neither body nor mind, took abstract shape. At first it was thought that everyone must have a separate individual Atman, but this idea breaks when the Atman is said to have no form, it being non-corporeal. That which has no form must be omnipresent. Time and space begin with the mind. The bodiless spirit which transcends the mind, must therefore be unlimited by time also. Time, space and causation go with the mind, and that which is above the mind must also be unlimited by these. Such being the nature of the spirit, how can we speak of it as a completely different entity in each person? In other words, to say that each person has a different Atman just like the body, is an absurdity. The spirit or the Atman must therefore be infinite and cannot be two, and so the common idea of your having one soul and I another, is an absurdity. The Real Man therefore is one—the infinite, omnipresent spirit—and the apparent man is only a limitation of that Real Man. This is what the ancient mythologies about the fall of man wanted to teach—that the man we experience now is the apparent man, and behind him is the Real Man, the omnipresent spirit.

30.3 THE UNIVERSAL SPIRIT IS THE REAL MAN

Thus man in his real nature is the Universal Being which is everywhere. People are frightened by this idea, because they think they thereby lose their individuality. On the other hand, reflection will reveal that by this they are only regaining their lost or forgotten individuality. If the claim of our present individuality is pressed to the logical conclusion, a thief should not aspire to be reformed and no man should change his habit, however undesirable. Individuality cannot also be confined to what we remember about ourselves. For we remember only very little about ourselves. In truth we are not individuals yet. We shall attain to true individuality only when we realise our nature as the Infinite Being—the being that cannot be divided, broken into bits. The apparent man is merely a struggle to express it, to manifest this real individuality. Evolution is not in the spirit. For the spirit, perfection is not a matter to be attained. It is already perfect. When this perfection is to be expressed through nature, the obstructive screens of nature have to be removed; the changes brought about thereby is only in the screen and not in what is behind. Evolution, therefore, is the clearing of certain obstructions of nature standing in the way of the manifestation of the spirit.

It is this perfection latent in man that makes him seek an ideal of perfection outside, either as a God or a perfect moral law or an ideal society. But perfection cannot ultimately be realised in the external. 'After long searches here and there, in temples and in churches, in earths and in heavens, at last you come back, completing the circle from where you started, to your own soul and find that He for whom you have been seeking all over the world, for whom you have been weeping and praying in churches and temples, on whom you were looking as the mystery of all mysteries shrouded in the clouds, is nearest of the near, is your own Self, the reality of your life, body, and soul. That is your own nature. Assert it, manifest it. ... It cannot be known. ... Were it knowable, it would not be what it is, for it is the eternal subject. Knowledge is a limitation, knowledge is objectifying. Knowledge is, as it were, a lower step. ... We are that eternal subject already; how can we know it?

30.4 WORLD-WELFARE AND SPIRITUAL REALISATION

The justification of all ethics lies in this spiritual nature of man. The central theme of ethics is self-abnegation—the sacrifice of the small self for the good of all. Man can really do so only when he has begun to see the one Self, his own Self, in all. Every act of self-sacrifice is a step towards this, towards the abandonment of the little self in favour of the one Universal Self. Utilitarianism, insisting on the material nature of man, can never bring any good ultimately. For 'As soon as I think that I am a little body, I want to preserve it, to protect it, to keep it nice, at the expense of other bodies; then you and I become separate. ... this idea of separation comes, it opens the door to all mischief and leads to all misery. This is the utility that if a very small fractional part of human beings living today can put aside the idea of selfishness, narrowness, and littleness, this earth will become a paradise tomorrow; but with machines and improvements of material knowledge only, it will never be. ... Without the knowledge of the Spirit, all material knowledge is only adding fuel to fire.'

Then the question arises whether it is practical to apply this truth in society. '*Truth does not pay homage to any society, ancient or modern. Society has to pay homage to Truth or die.* ... Is nothing practical but pounds, shillings, and p:nce? If so, why boast of your society? *That society is the greatest, where the highest truths become practical.* ... if society is not fit for the highest truths, make it so; and the sooner, the better. Stand up, men and women, in this spirit, dare to believe in the Truth, dare to practice the Truth! ... The world requires a few hundred bold men and women. Practise that boldness which dares know the Truth, which dares show the Truth in life, which does not quake before death, nay, welcomes death, makes a man know that he, is the Spirit, that, in the whole universe, nothing can kill him. Then you will be free. Then you will know yours real Soul.'

31

MAYA AND ILLUSION

The doctrine of maya forms one of the pillars of the
Vedanta philosophy. It is, however, often misinterpreted
to mean illusion. Although by usage the word might
have got some such sense in the course of the evolution
of the doctrine, in Vedanta proper its meaning is not il-
lusoriness of the world. In the *Rigveda* it is said ' "Indra
through his Maya assumed various forms." ' In this
earliest use of the word, it might have meant 'magical'
spell. The word does not appear in any other meaning
for long, but next we come across the idea of a mist that
covers reality and prevents us from knowing it. Much
later, the word maya reappears in the *Svetasvatara Upanishad*, where it is identified with nature: ' "Know nature to be Maya and the Ruler of this Maya is the Lord
Himself." ' It was in the hands of Buddhist thinkers
that the word got the peculiar slant towards illusionism.
There was a section of Buddhists, the *Vijnanavadins*, who

maintained that ideas alone are there, not the external objects corresponding to them. They considered the experience of the world outside as maya, illusory perception, the ideas alone being real. This is the philosophy of idealism. But the Maya of the Vedanta, in its last developed form, is neither Idealism nor Realism, nor is it a theory. It is a simple statement of facts—what we are and what we see around us.' We are taken up with external nature, which is the most real of all real things for us. Modern science is an expression of man's faith in the external world and his hope that its investigation will help him understand the very nature of things, which we call the ultimate truth. But this cannot be for the following reasons: (1) The Vedanta points out that our investigation of nature is limited by our mind and its associated faculties, the senses. (2) Mind is limited by space, time and causation, which form its warp and woof, and no one can jump out of it and understand things without its mediation. (3) The world which we actually experience therefore exists only in relation to the minds that experience it as such. If we have less or more senses than we actually possess, we shall be seeing the world in a different manner. The world experienced externally has therefore no unchangeable and ultimate existence. But it cannot be called nonexistent, because it is experienced.

31.2 THE WORLD—A MEETING OF CONTRADICTIONS
AND THEREFORE INEXPLICABLE

'Now, it is a statement of fact that this world is a Tantalus's hell, that we do not know anything about this universe, yet at the same time we cannot say that we do not know. ... This standing between knowledge and ignorance, this mystic twilight, the mingling of truth and falsehood—and where they meet—no one knows. We are walking in the midst of a dream, half sleeping, half waking, passing all our lives in a haze; this is the fate of everyone of us. This is the fate of all sense-knowledge. This is the fate of all philosophy, of all boasted science, of all boasted human knowledge. ... What you call matter, or spirit, or mind, or anything else you may like to call them, the fact remains the same: we cannot say that they are, we cannot say that they are not. We cannot say they are one, we cannot say they are many. This eternal play of light and darkness—indiscriminate, indistinguishable, inseparable—is always there. A fact, yet at the same time not a fact; awake and at the same time asleep. This is a statement of facts, and this is what is called Maya. We are born in this Maya, we live in it, we think in it, we dream in it. We are philosophers in it, we are spiritual men in it, nay, we are devils in this Maya, and we are gods in this Maya. Stretch your ideas as far as you can make them higher and higher, call them infinite or by any other name you please, even these ideas are within this Maya. It cannot be otherwise, and the whole of human knowledge is a generalization of this Maya trying to know it as it appears to be. This is the work of Nāma-Rupa—name and form. Everything that has form, everything that calls up an idea in your mind, is within Maya; for everything that is bound by the laws of time, space, and causation is within Maya.'

Thus the world of our experience is a mixture of contradictions, of facts and fiction, of the permanent and the impermanent, of the existent and the non-existent. It is this contradictory incomprehensible nature of the world that is indicated by the term maya.

31.3 ANALYSIS OF THE CONDITIONS OF LIFE TO SHOW THE CONTRADICTIONS

An examination of the facts and experiences of life will show how they are riddled with contradictions and are thus a mixture of fact and fiction. We want to know everything and try to think problems to their final solution; but as we proceed we find an adamantine wall, and we soon find ourselves wandering in a circle of thought, coming to the same position from which we started. The higher voice in us is urging us always to be good, but practical necessity always compels us to be selfish. Most people are optimists when they start life, but they are compelled to become pessimists in the end. There is the tremendous fact of death which no man, however highly placed or wise, can avoid. And yet everyone clings to life as if it were going to last forever. A mother dotes on her child and brings it up; probably when he comes to manhood, he persecutes her and yet the mother cannot shake off her attachment to him. Everyone is after the Golden Fleece, but a reasonable man also knows that his chances are perhaps one in twenty million. A reformer seeks to remedy the evils of society, though he knows full well that several such reformers had worked before him, and that before they had finished their reform, abuses even greater than what they tried to remedy had come up. Social evils are like chronic rheumatism or like an old building. You drive away the rheumatism from one part of the body, soon it comes up in another part; or you repair a very old house in one place, but in another place it begins to fall down. It is said Christianity is the true religion, because Christian nations are prosperous and powerful. But this prosperity has been attained largely by the extermination and enslavement of non-Christian nations, which in themselves contradicts all axioms of religion. Prosperity in one place means poverty in another. Animals live upon plants, men live on animals, and strong men on the weak. It is said good will come in course of time, as the evil subsides. We do not, however, find any signs of it as yet, and besides, why should it at all be achieved in this diabolical way—that it should come through the sufferings of countless millions? Those who are really progressing know that the more we progress, the more avenues arc open to pain as well as to pleasure. The primitive man had none of the sufferings of the modern civilised man. He stood physical pains well and he had no sufferings arising from mental tensions. The physical insecurities and privations he was exposed to have been overcome by modern civilisation, but in their place civilisation has made him subject to much intenser sufferings from a host of subtle and insidious circumstances. And yet sophistication is considered the way to happiness.

It is this state of tremendous contradictoriness of life's hopes and experiences that the Vedantin wants to convey by the concept of maya. 'Maya is not a theory for the explanation of the world; it is simply a statement of facts as they exist, that the very basis of our being is contradiction, that everywhere we have to move through this tremendous contradiction, that wherever there is good, there must also be evil, and wherever there is evil, there must be some good, wherever there is life, death must follow as its shadow, and everyone who smiles will have to weep, and vice versa. Nor can this state of things be remedied ... for the conditions will remain the same.'

31.4 PERFECTIONISM:
AN UNREALISABLE PHILOSOPHY

Some German philosophers have propounded a theory that the Infinite is trying to express itself in this universe, that a time will come when the Infinite will succeed in doing so, and that everything will be all right then. But the question has to be answered whether the finite can ever express the Infinite fully. For the Absolute and the Infinite can become the universe only by limitation. Everything that comes through the intellect or the mind or the senses must be limited, and for the limited to be the unlimited is manifest absurdity. On the other hand the Vedanta also admits that the Infinite is trying to express itself in the finite, but that there will come a time when, finding that this is an impossibility, it will beat a retreat. This beating the retreat means renunciation, which is the beginning of real religion. The mind learns the lesson that desires are never conquered through the satisfaction of desires; only they increase thereby, like fire when ghee is poured in it.

Does it mean that we need not work for the improvement of life, for the eradication of the sufferings of others? The implication is just the opposite. That is the only way we can ourselves make spiritual progress and do some limited good to others; but this philosophy will eliminate fanaticism from reformers and revolutionaries on account of the awareness of the inherent limitation of their efforts, and thus make them level-headed and patient, and help them realise some good in place of wasting their energies in hatred and impatience.

31.5 VEDANTA HAS NO COMPROMISE WITH AGNOSTICISM

At this stage agnosticism lifts its voice and says that as we are in a world that is incomprehensible and irreme-diable, let us take it for what it is worth and enjoy it with-out any thought of the ultimate nature of things. But this is advocating slavery to nature, which the Vedanta says is the denial of the higher destiny of man. Life in nature is no doubt incomprehensible and is a matter of contradictions, but man can rise above nature and get out of its irremediable contradictions. He can be free. All the religions of the world are the assertion of the prospect of this freedom for him. Even in the lowest forms of religion consisting in the worship of ancestors and of gruesome spirits, this aspiration for freedom is found; for, man finds in these beings, entities with greater freedom and control over nature than himself. This ideal of freedom becomes better articulated in the idea of a personal God who is beyond the limita-tion of maya, who controls and directs maya. It comes to be believed that through adoration of Him and His grace, we can attain to freedom from nature. Most of the great religions stop their speculation with this. But the Vedanta goes further. With the Vedantist 'The idea grows and grows until the Vedantist finds that He who, he thought, was standing outside, is he himself and is in reality within. He is the one who is free, but who through limitation thought he was bound.'

32

MAYA AND THE EVOLUTION OF
THE CONCEPTION OF GOD

32.1 GODS GROW WITH MAN

In most of the ancient religions, we get gods, who are only powerful beings without any ethical sublimity about them. They often did things that are repugnant even to men. They drank, they fought, they sought possessions and indulged in sex. In spite of their unethical character, however, the men who worshipped them found nothing incongruous in their character. But people of today would criticize those worshippers and their objects of worship, and wonder how those ancients worshipped these gods at all. This attitude arises from the non-recognition of the fact that, just as the ancient man has developed into the modern man with new intellectual standards and ethical norms, the gods too have grown. The evolution of the worshipper is recognised but not that of the worshipped. Man grows, and correspondingly his idea of God also grows. It may look incongruous to say that God grows. The puzzle is solved when we remember that what is growing is man's idea of God according to his own development. The reality behind the conception of God does not change, so too the real man does not change. It is human nature that changes. When change reveals more and more of the facts behind, it is called progression; when it hides, it is called retrogression. Thus as we grow, the gods too grow. Just as we reveal ourselves with our growth, so the gods reveal themselves until thought reaches the stage of monotheism—the theory of the one God, the God of gods, who is the creator and master of the world, and who answers to the highest ethical demands of the human heart in respect of goodness, justice and mercy. In Christian thought also, the Jehovah who displaced all the other Molochs, grows gradually from a ferocious deity into the Father in Heaven.

32.2 THE ETHICAL PROBLEM
FACED BY MONOTHEISM

The idea of such a personal God as the explanation of life, brings man immediately into confrontation with the problem of evil. In the primitive religions having gods without any moral halo about them, the difficulty was not felt very much. The natural man probably did not question the 'why' of things, but took the world of experience for granted. But as man became sophisticated and sought refuge in an omniscient, omnipotent and morally perfect God, the question came why there should be disharmony, suffering and evil in a world created by a good and omnipotent God. The ethical norm was no doubt of very slow development. In the human mind there are naturally the two impulses of 'do' and 'do not' with regard to the things of sensate life. The 'do not' may be very, weak at first. The first represents *pravritti* and the 'do not' *nivritti*. Religion commences with the latter, when man begins to feel some inhibition against leading a purely instinctive life, against being a mere creature of the senses. Along with that, a little love arises in the heart, prompting him to move away from self-centredness. Thus the love of the family and the tribe, a sense of duty towards them, springs up in the heart. When these noble ideas arose, a glimpse of something higher, more ethical, dawned before the eyes of man. The old gods, boisterous, fighting, drinking and delighting in sacrifices, became incongruous in his eyes, and an ethical, just, loving and adorable universal Father God came, either to absorb the earlier conceptions or to displace them.

But the thoughtful mind of man could not rest with this even. For, he began to realise that, just as the old gods were incongruous with the ideal of a Father God, the same incongruity persisted between Him and the world of His creation. If the conception of God got refined in arithmetical progression, the difficulty and doubt about His compatibility with the world increased in geometrical progression. The question arose why under the reign of an almighty and all-loving God, who is also the creator of the universe, diabolical things should be allowed to remain. Where is the loving and merciful God? Does He not see that millions and millions of men and animals are perishing? Is He not aware of the degradation of human nature in slums and in morally depressing situations? ... We may shut our eyes to all these things, but that would be emulating the ostrich, hiding our heads from the reality of the situation—a hideous world which is nothing better than the hell of Tantalus. Unhappiness is the fate of those who are content to live in the world, confining their interest to the body and the senses. A thousand times worse is the fate of those who dare to stand forth for truth and for higher things, who dare to ask for something higher than mere brute existence here. To say that ultimately good will come out of these evils is no explanation. If we suppose that it is a personal God like a human being who made everything, these so-called explanations and theories, which try to prove that out of evil comes good, are insufficient and unsatisfactory. Let twenty thousand good things come but why should they come from evil when a good and merciful personal God is presiding over it all? The question remains unanswered, and it will remain always so. The philosophy of India was compelled to admit this.

32.3 THE IMPERSONAL ABSOLUTE

In societies outside India where monotheistic thought came to prevail, the old gods were suppressed, and all criticisms of monotheistic ideas were answered by dogmatism and by persecution organised by the church and the state. But in India there was freedom of thought, and philosophical and religious problems were allowed to be settled by debate and discussion based on insight. The Upanishadic thinkers knew that the primitive gods and the monotheistic God were not reconcilable with the ethical notions of later times, and that the criticisms of the atheists contained a good deal of truth. But they faced the situation neither by joining the atheists nor by condemning them. They accepted all trends of thought and all theologies as versions of the Truth struggling to express itself through inadequate language, and so they sought to discover that Truth through reflection and abstract meditation. The result was the Vedanta philosophy, in which out of the old deities and out of the monotheistic God or the ruler of the universe, they developed a yet higher idea in what is called the impersonal Absolute. They found oneness throughout the Universe. 'He who sees in this world of manifoldness

that One running through all, in this world of death he
who finds that One Infinite Life, and in this world of
insentience and ignorance he who finds that One Light
and Knowledge, unto him belongs eternal peace. Unto
none else, unto none else.'

33

MAYA AND FREEDOM

Life is a battlefield. Victorious or defeated, its final end is death. Man comes out of his childhood with hope but he finds nature standing as an adamantine wall; the further he goes, the further recedes the ideal till death relieves him of the struggle. A scientist, eager to know the secrets of nature, discovers law after law, applies them to practical life, and achieves great results and much praise. But his achievements are a trifle and fall into insignificance before the forces of nature, which are every day doing all this on a tremendously vaster scale without any of that fanfare of the scientist. Man rushes for pleasures to sense objects, but he is only crippled and cheated ultimately. We go on investigating nature's mysteries with our intellect, but after we have taken a few steps, we find the beginningless and endless wall of space and time blocking our progress. With every breath and pulsation of the heart we feel we are free, but in fact we find ourselves nature's bond slaves only. Every

mother thinks her child is a born genius or will grow
to be the best of men, but he perhaps turns a drunkard
and ill-treats her, and yet she dotes on him and covers
her attachment with a mass of flowers calling it love.

33.2 THE TWO VOICES AND THEIR TWO WAYS OPEN
TO MAN: *PRAVRITTI* AND *NIVRITTI*

Thus, frustration and death, of which nature's
adamantine wall of human thraldom is constructed,
face him on all sides. Two ways have been suggested
to meet this situation. The first is the way of practical
wisdom. It says, ' "Make hay while the sun shines," as
the proverb says. It is all true, it is a fact, but do not
mind it. Seize the few pleasures you can. ... "Take the
world as it is; sit down as calmly and comfortably as you
can and be contented with all these miseries. When you
receive blows, say they are not blows but flowers; and
when you are driven about like slaves, say that you are
free. Day and night tell lies to others and to your own
souls, because that is the only way to live happily." '
The other way is suggested by the voice of the spirit.
'True it is that we are all slaves of Maya, born in Maya,
and live in Maya ... That we are all miserable, that this
world is really a prison, that even our so-called trailing
beauty is but a prison-house, and that even our intellects
and minds are prison-houses, have been known for ages

upon ages.' But it does not mean there is no way out. We find that with all this, with these terrible facts before us, in the midst of sorrow and suffering, even in this world where life and death are synonymous, even here, there is a still small voice that is ringing through all ages, through every country and in every heart: "This My Maya is divine, made up of qualities, and very difficult to cross. Yet those that come unto Me, cross the river of life"' (*Gita*); or "Come unto Me all ye that labour and are heavy laden and I will give you rest." (*Bible*). This is the voice that is leading us forward. Man has heard it, and is hearing it all through the ages. This voice comes to men when everything seems to be lost and hope has fled, when man's dependence on his own strength has been crushed down, and everything seems to melt away between his fingers, and life is a hopeless ruin. Then he hears it. This is called religion.'

33.3 RELIGION IS THE VOICE OF FREEDOM

A curious fact that emerges when we introspect is that in spite of the shackles of bondage, we cannot help feeling this call of freedom from the recesses of our being. At every step we are knocked down, as it were, by maya, and shown that we are bound, and yet simultaneously comes the inner voice asserting our freedom. 'All human life, all nature, therefore, is struggling to attain to freedom. The sun is moving towards the goal, so is the earth in circling round the sun, so is the moon in circling round the earth. To that goal the planet is moving, and the air is blowing. Everything is struggling towards that. The saint is going towards that voice—he cannot help it, it is no glory to him. So is the sinner. The charitable man is going straight towards that voice, and cannot be hindered; the miser is also going towards the same destination: the greatest worker of good hears the same voice within, and he cannot resist it, he must go towards the voice; so with the most arrant idler. One stumbles more than another, and him who stumbles more we call bad, him who stumbles less we call good. '

Now applying this idea of freedom to religion, all religions, even the crude forms of it, represent man's quest for freedom from slavery to nature. In ancestor worship or in the worship of powerful and cruel deities, the primitive man worships beings who have much greater control over nature than himself, and could do such things as flying up in the air or passing through barriers, which are beyond his power. He finds in them a reflection of his aspiration to be free from nature. But his own ideas of nature are not very clear. As man's mind develops, his ideas of nature also expand; so too his ideas of the deity. He arrives at the idea of the one God, monotheism, which holds there is maya (nature) and there is a Being who is the ruler of this maya, who is not only free from the bonds of maya but is also controller or possessor, and who can free man subject to maya, from that bondage.

Here then monotheism ends, and Vedanta begins. Vedanta accepts this idea but it holds that it is still a partial vision of the Truth. It is not 'Nearer my God to Thee', but 'Nearer my God to me.' The idea of God as an extra- cosmic being, beyond nature, attracting us all towards Him, has to be brought nearer and nearer, without degrading or degenerating it. 'The God of heaven becomes the God in nature, and the God in nature becomes the God who is nature, and the God who is nature becomes the God within this temple of the body, and the God dwelling in the temple of the body at last becomes the temple itself, becomes the soul and man— and there it reaches the last words it can teach. He whom the sages have been seeking in all these places is in our own hearts; the voice that you heard was right, says the Vedanta, but the direction you gave to the voice was wrong. That ideal of freedom that you perceived was correct, but you projected it outside yourself, and that was your mistake. Bring it nearer and nearer, until you find that it was all the time within you, it was the Self of your own self. That freedom was your own nature, and this Maya never bound you. Nature never has power over you. Like a frightened child you were dreaming that it was throttling you, and the release from this fear is the goal: not only to see it intellectually, but to perceive it, actualise it, much more definitely than we perceive this world.'

THE ABSOLUTE AND THE MANIFESTATION

34.1 CAN THE ABSOLUTE BECOME THE RELATIVE?

The most difficult question answered in the Advaita philosophy is how the Absolute has become the finite. The contents of the question may be analysed thus: (1) Here is on the one hand, the Absolute, without time, space or causation, without any trace of plurality. (2) On the other band, here is the world of plurality which includes not only the material world but the mental and the spiritual worlds, heaven and earth and everything that exists. (3) This plurality is the expression of the Absolute. (4) This transformation is accomplished by the Absolute coming through, or appearing through the mediation of time, space and causation, which in themselves cannot in any way be conceived as existing in the Absolute itself. Causation is succession of events, and succession requires time and space. They go together and we are compelled to understand by the necessity of thought that they came 'after ... the degeneration of the Absolute into the phenomenal, and not before.'

The question 'why' or 'how' also assumes that nothing is independent, that everything is being acted upon by something outside of itself. *Interdependence* is the law of the whole universe while *independence is* the nature of the Absolute.

In the light of this analysis of the problem, we find that the question how or why the Absolute has become the relative is absurd and illogical. This is a question that can be put only in regard to the phenomenal world of plurality where interdependence or the cause and effect relation is the rule. For, as already stated, cause and effect assume a succession of events, and succession assumes time and space. Thus, a question that is relevant only in regard interdependent entities that are of the phenomenal world, is asked about the Absolute, which is by the very conception is non-phenomenal, to which the concepts of space, time and causation are not applicable. In fact what the questioner expects is to give an answer about the Absolute in terms of the categories of time, space and causation that are applicable only to the phenomenal or the world of plurality. The question is thus absurd and therefore incapable of being answered in logical concepts.

Now supposing someone gives an answer to it. The implication of any answer would be to limit the Absolute by our mind. When the Absolute is thus limited, it ceases to be the Absolute; the very attempt at answer-

ing it reduces it to a limited category within the phenomenal world. That is why Schopenhauer's idea of
equating the will with the Absolute and speaking of the
will as this cause of the universe is a failure and causes
great confusion in his philosophy. Will is something
changeable, and therefore cannot come over the line
drawn above time, space and causation. Besides, will,
as we understand it, manifests in consciousness, and
is thus a later product. It cannot therefore be equated
with the Absolute.

34.2 THE KNOWN AND THE UNKNOWN

Hence the question 'how' and 'why' the Absolute
has become the finite world of plurality has never been
answered satisfactorily. The question is a logical absurdity, and all attempted answers are equally absurd in a
logical sense. The wisest of men have therefore maintained that the Absolute is unknown and is unknowable.
But this statement is not meant to convey the meaning
that agnostics give to these expressions. The agnostics
mean by the expressions, the 'unknown' and the 'unknowable', that the ultimate nature of things cannot be
understood in any sense, that questions about it should
be ignored as of a non-existent problem, and man must
concern himself with the relative world as the be-all
and end-all of existence. The Vedantin uses the terms

'unknown' and 'unknowable' in the very opposite sense of the agnostics. He means that the Absolute or God is something more intimate than objects classified as known and knowable. 'This chair is known, but God is intensely more than that, because in and through Him we have to know this chair itself. He is the Witness, the eternal Witness of all knowledge. Whatever we know we have to know in and through Him. He is the Essence of our own Self. He is the Essence of this ego, this I and we cannot know anything excepting in and through that I. ... Thus God is infinitely nearer to us than the chair, but yet He is infinitely higher. ... Neither known, nor unknown, but something infinitely higher than either. He is your Self. ... in and through Him we exist. Not the He is standing somewhere and making my blood circulate. What is meant is that He is the Essence of all this, the Soul of my soul. You cannot by any possibility say you know Him ... You cannot get out of yourself, so you cannot know Him. Knowledge is objectification. ... This cannot be done with God, because He is the Essence of our souls. ... Here is one of the profoundest passages in Vedanta: "He that is the Essence of your soul, He is the Truth, He is the Self, thou art That, O Shvetaketu." This is what is meant by "Thou art God." You cannot describe Him by any other language. All attempts of language, calling Him father, or brother, or our dearest friend, are attempts to objectify God, which cannot be done. He is the Eternal Subject of everything. I am the subject of this chair; I see the chair; so God is the Eternal Subject of my soul. How can you objectify Him, the Essence of your souls, the Reality of everything? Thus, I would repeat to you once more, God is neither knowable nor unknowable, but something infinitely higher than either ... You cannot know your own self; you cannot move it out and make it an object to look at, because you *are* that and cannot separate yourself from it. Neither is it unknowable, for what is better known than yourself? It is really the centre of our knowledge. In exactly the same sense, God is neither unknowable nor known, but infinitely higher than both; for He is our real Self.'

34.3 THE ABSOLUTE IN RELATION TO TIME, SPACE AND CAUSATION

There are still more elements of absurdity in speaking of the Absolute manifesting through the medium of time, space and causation as the world of multiplicity. To say that the Absolute manifests through time, space and causality, we have to assume that these are two different entities, the Absolute on one side, and the manifesting medium on the other. They have to be taken as uncaused existences, which is absurd from the point of view of Advaita. There cannot be two independent existences without each limiting the other. This destroys the very concept of the Absolute. The Absolute is unique; it can only be One without a second. So time, space and causation cannot have an independent status even when these three are taken together as a unified category. In their very nature also these three are found to have no existence in themselves, but in a relative sense only. Time is dependent on our state of mind. In sleep it vanishes; in dream its standard has wide variations. Besides, time cannot be thought of in abstraction. It is experienced only in relation to two events. So also space can be thought of only as within limits, or as coloured or occupied by something. As for causation, it is felt only in relation to two events in succession and is therefore dependent on space and time. So, extraneously these can be conceived only as a kind of existence dependent on the Absolute, and intrinsically as mutually dependent existences. They have not even the degree of existence which a chair or a wall has. They are shadows around everything without substantiality. They have no real existence, but yet are not non-existent, seeing that through them all things are manifesting as this universe.

An analogy can be found in the relation of the ocean and the waves. The Absolute is the ocean and all the beings included in the universe are like waves. The wave is basically one with the ocean and not different from it. It takes on name and form in the frame-work of time as cause and effect, and soon loses its distinctiveness again when it subsides in the ocean. Space and time, which gave it shape, seem to be entirely dependent on the wave, as their experience is strictly in relation to the wave, and just like the form itself, they have no relevance when the wave subsides. The wave itself is entirely dependent on water, and only water is left when its limitation of space and time is gone. Thus, in this example, water alone has an absolute ontological status, and the wave and its framework of time, space and causation are experienced for a moment as dependent existences and pass away immediately. They cannot be given the same ontological status. They are experienced, and as such they cannot be called entirely 'non-existent', but yet they cannot be called also 'existent' in the sense water is existent, they being dependent and ephemeral. In the same way the Absolute only appears as waves of this ocean, of plurality called the world, to a centre of consciousness included among these waves. The water is water itself all the while it is appearing as the waves. This capacity of appearing as the limited without actually transforming and losing one's entity is maya. 'As soon as the wave goes, they vanish. As soon as the individual gives up this Maya, it vanishes for him and he becomes free. '

34.4 MEANING OF EVOLUTION

Now all evolution is meaningful only in the sense of the individual struggling to discover his Absolute nature. The environment is the obstacle, and the individual, who is the Absolute in reality, is struggling to his absolute potential. We cannot possibly overcome all aspects of the environment as such, although we may manipulate it considerably. So all through nature we find that conquest of environment comes very largely by changes in the subject. For example the fish wants to overcome its enemies in the water; it accomplishes this not by changing the water but by developing wings and becoming a bird. Applying this to religion and morality we find that the conquest of evil can ultimately come by a change in the subject alone. Thus the Advaita system lays all its force on the subjective side of man. All religion, morality, discipline and work become spiritually significant to the extent they help this inner transformation of man.

34.5 ADVAITA AS THE SCIENTIFIC
AND UNIVERSAL RELIGION

The Advaita is the only religious philosophy that can attract a scientific mind. The old dualistic theories do not satisfy such a mind, because 'A man must have not only faith, but intellectual faith too.' It saved India twice: once when the Buddha preached it to the masses and next when Sankara perfected its intellectual framework. If there is any doctrine that can save the scientific west today from materialism, it is the rationalistic religion of oneness, Advaita, with its doctrine of an impersonal God. 'It comes whenever religion seems to disappear and irreligion seems to prevail, and that is why it has taken ground in Europe and America. ... We want today that bright sun of intellectuality joined with the heart of Buddha, the wonderful infinite heart of love and mercy. This union will give us the highest philosophy. Science and religion will meet and shake hands. Poetry and philosophy will become friends. This will be the religion of the future, and if we can work it out, we may be sure that it will be for all times and peoples.'

Another great feature of Advaita, so much needed today, is that it is non-destructive. It helps everyone to get higher and higher, because of its all-inclusiveness. 'This philosophy preaches a God who is a sum total. If you seek a universal religion which can apply to everyone, that religion must not be composed of only the parts, but it must always be their sum total and include all degrees of religious development.' A dualist by the very presupposition of his thought has necessarily got to condemn all others who differ from him. But the Advaitin has no quarrel with the dualists who, he accepts, is on the right track, provided he is sincere in his faith. It is a constitutional necessity of the dualists to see the many. The Advaitin, however, knows that whatever his theory, he is going towards the same goal as himself. But if the dualistic ideas are not enlightened by the higher thought of Vedanta, it leads to many undesirable consequences. Some dualists are forced to think that God has some favourites. Others become narrow enough to say that all except those who follow their doctrine are going to be damned, and some go to the extent of practising this in this world itself by instituting persecutions and holy wars. Many dualistic faiths preach a God who is a big magistrate with a rod in hand and enforces His ethics by threats of punishment.

Doctrines that generate this type of narrow and exclusive mentality are not consistent with this age of science and intermingling of cultures. What is now wanted is a combination of the greatest heart with the greatest intellect, of infinite love with infinite knowledge. The Vedanta with its impersonal God with only three indicating attributes—Infinite Existence, Infinite Knowledge, Infinite Bliss—is the remedy for correcting all one-sidedness and exclusiveness in religion.

GOD IN EVERYTHING

35.1 TRUE MEANING OF RENUNCIATION

Our life in this world is cast in the midst of evil. From time without beginning men have been trying to remedy this in their own way. But the remedy often results in subtler evils. Religions tell us that there is life beyond this world of evil. It is the Infinite—call it God, Allah, Jehovah or by other names that have no religious significance. Religions therefore seem to propose that this world of evil is nothing, and beyond it is something that is very real and all good. Therefore, this world with its obvious and irremediable evil is to be given up. That seems to be the suggestion of religions as understood ordinarily. But this looks like killing a mosquito sitting on a person by giving a blow that kills no doubt the mosquito, but also the man along with it. 'If we understand the giving up of the world in its old, crude sense, then it would come to this: that we must not work, that we must be idle, sitting like lumps of earth, neither thinking nor doing anything, but must become fatalists,

driven about by every circumstance, ordered about by
the laws of nature, drifting from place to place.'

But this is not the real meaning of giving up the
world. The counsel of Vedanta is not a piece of dry sui-
cidal advice. It consists in deification of the world—giving up the world as we think of it, as it appears to us,
and knowing it as it really is. We are to deify it and see
it as God alone. So the Isopanishad says: ' "Whatever
exists in this universe is to be covered with the Lord." '
What is therefore meant by abandonment is the transformation of outlook. It is not that one should abandon
one's wife and children in a brutal manner, but one
has to see that they are divine in essence, which is possible only when one's possessiveness arising from one's
self-centred outlook is given up. 'What existed was the
Lord Himself. It is He who is in the child, in the wife,
and in the husband; it is He who is in the good and in
the bad; He is in the sin and in the sinner; He is in life
and in death.'

Do not desire anything and do not possess anything—this does not mean, be like a wall or an inani-
mate object. It means only to know the truth about
wealth. 'Wealth does not belong to anybody. Have no
idea of proprietorship, possessorship. You are nobody,
nor am I, nor anyone else. All belongs to the Lord, because the opening verse (of the Isopanishad) told us to
put the Lord in everything. God is in the wealth that

you enjoy. He is in the desire that rises in your mind. He is in the things you buy to satisfy your desire; He is in your beautiful attire, in your beautiful ornaments. This is the line of thought. All will be metamorphosed as soon as you begin to see things in that light. If you put God in your every movement, in your conversation, in your form, in everything, the whole scene changes, and the world, instead of appearing as one of woe and misery, will become a heaven.'

35.2 WITNESS ATTITUDE

The real enjoyment comes when you are only an on-looker and not a participant. In a place where pictures are exhibited, the persons engaged in selling and buy-ing are not the real enjoyers. Real enjoyment is got by the onlooker who is there with the idea of seeing and not possessing. 'this whole universe is a picture, and when these desires have vanished, men will enjoy the world, and then this buying and selling and these foolish ideas of possession will be ended. The money-lender gone, the buyer gone, the seller gone, this world remains the picture, a beautiful painting. I never read of any more beautiful conception of God than the following: "He is the Great Poet, the Ancient Poet; the whole universe is His poem, coming in verses and rhymes and rhythms, written in infinite bliss." When we have given up de-

sires, then alone shall we be able to read and enjoy this
universe of God. Then everything will become deified.
Nooks and corners, by-ways and shady places, which
we thought dark and unholy, will be all deified. They
will all reveal their true nature, and we shall smile at
ourselves and think that all this weeping and crying
has been but child's play, and we were only standing
by, watching.'

'Desire to live a hundred years. ... Have the desire to
live a long life of helpfulness, of blissfulness and activity on this earth. Thus working, you will find the way
out. There is no other way. If a man plunges headlong
into foolish luxuries of the world without knowing the
truth, he has missed his footing, he cannot reach the
goal. And if a man curses the world, goes into a forest,
mortifies his flesh, and kills himself little by little by
starvation, makes his heart a barren waste, kills out
all feelings, and becomes harsh, stern, and dried-up,
that man also has missed the way. These are the two
extremes, the two mistakes at either end. Both have lost
the way, both have missed the goal.'

'So work, says the Vedanta, putting God in everything, and knowing Him to be in everything. Work
incessantly, holding life as something deified, as God
Himself, and knowing that this is all we have to do, this
is all we should ask for. God is in everything, where else
shall we go to find Him? He is already in every work,

in every thought, in every feeling. Thus knowing, we must work—this is the only way, there is no other. Thus the effects of work will not bind us. We have seen how false desires are the cause of all the misery and evil we suffer, but when they are thus deified, purified, through God, they bring no evil, they bring no misery. Those who have not learnt this secret will have to live in a demoniacal world until they discover it. ... What is a demoniacal world? The Vedanta says, ignorance.'

35.3 THE PRACTICAL USE OF THE ABOVE IDEAS

It will be objected that this ideal of seeing God in everything is nice to talk about. But when we try to practise it, we find it impossible to do so. When we are up against worldly situations, we forget all this and become agitated by our earth-bound emotions. It is like the case of a stag, which was admiring his fine figure reflected in water and boasting to its young one of its strength. But immediately it heard the barking of dogs, it forgot all about its strength and ran for its life. After a long time when it returned gasping, and was asked why it ran away, it replied that when it hears the barking of dogs, it cannot stand still. Such is a man's condition in the world in the face of the dogs of worldly passion and trying situations. All this is true, yet it gives us an ideal to strive for, and to have an ideal is far better than to have none and grope in the darkness of life. If a man with an ideal makes a thousand mistakes, the man without any makes them in millions. To have an ideal means to be striving always, and that is the only condition of growth. The self-complacent man with no ideal to strive for is in a stagnant condition. He never grows, because he is satisfied with his predicament. The man with an ideal is not discouraged by failures. He may fail but he will still strive, knowing that failures are the stepping stones to success. Thought is the main propelling force within us. So the mind must be filled with the highest thoughts that the Vedanta offers, and we must reflect and meditate upon it constantly, so that our mind gets saturated with these high thoughts.

The great thought that the Vedanta places before us is the unity of all existence. It demonstrates that all our misery comes through ignorance, and that this ignorance is responsible for our perception of multiplicity in place of the unity and the consequent miseries of life. So we have to trace 'the reality of everything, the secret of everything. Where is there any more misery for him? What does he desire? He has traced the reality of everything to the Lord, the Centre, the Unity of everything, and that is Eternal Existence, Eternal Knowledge, Eternal Bliss. Neither death nor disease, nor sorrow, nor misery, nor discontent is there. All is Perfect Union and Perfect Bliss. For whom should he mourn then? In the Reality, there is no death, there is no misery; in the Reality, there is no one to mourn for, no one to be sorry for. He has penetrated everything, the Pure One, the Formless, the Bodiless, the Stainless. He the Knower, He the Great Poet, the Self-Existent, He who is giving to everyone what he deserves. They grope in darkness who worship this ignorant world, the world that is produced out of ignorance, thinking of it as Existence, and those who live their whole lives in this world, and never find anything better or higher, are groping in still greater darkness. But he who knows the secret of nature, seeing That which is beyond nature through the help of nature, he crosses death, and through the help of That which is beyond nature, he enjoys Eternal Bliss. "Thou sun, who hast covered the Truth with thy golden disc, do thou remove the veil, so that I may see the Truth that is within thee. I have known the Truth that is within thee, I have known what is the real meaning of thy rays and thy glory and have seen That which shines in thee; the Truth in thee I see, and That which is within thee is within me, and I am That."

36

REALISATION

Man's philosophical enquiry was at first directed outward. He was interested to know who created the world, and why He created it. The answer he got was at best the idea of a personal governor of the universe; a human being immensely magnified, but yet to all intents and purposes, a human being. This is only a partial explanation at the best. We see the universe as human beings, and our God is only our human explanation of the universe. If cows were philosophers, they would have had a 'cow universe' and a 'cow solution' of the problem. Moreover we apprehend the universe only through the five senses, and higher beings with still subtler faculties will find the universe and its explanation different from our understanding of them. Hence the necessity of a solution that is applicable to all points of view. For this, we have to go into the depths of our own consciousness. The sphere of external perceptions is like the circumference of a circle with innumerable points of view. But if we can go to the centre of our being, we get at a vantage ground that is the centre or substratum of the whole universe. It was a discovery of the ancient sages of India that the centre of our being is the centre of the universe too. All planets gravitate towards that one point, and that is the common ground for finding a common solution for the mystery of the universe.

This is the meaning of the doctrine of realisation held forth in the Vedantic tradition. No one can discover the God of the universe by going into the skies or other planets or anywhere outside. Though His glory is manifest everywhere, He is discovered as spirit, the ultimate basis of everything, only if we approach Him through the innermost gateway of our Self, the centre and substratum of our being.

This is the great lesson that the *Kathopanishad* wants to convey though its figurative conversation between *Yama* and Nachiketa. Being disgusted with the hypocritical conduct of the father in performing a fake sacrificial rite, the boy put unpleasant questions to the father, who on being annoyed, asked the boy to get away to the realm of *Yama*, the god of death. The boy goes there, and *Yama* being pleased with him offers him three boons. The first and the second boon selected by him related to the welfare of his own father and knowledge about certain sacrificial rites. The third boon he wanted was to be told about the real nature of man—whether anything in him continues to exist

hereafter or whether everything ends with death. The
god of death in order to test him tries to tempt him with
power, wealth and enjoyment. But Nachiketa rejects
them all and sticks to his choice of knowledge about
the real nature of man.

Pleased with him, *Yama* tells, congratulating Nachiketa: ' "Perfection is one thing and enjoyment another;
these two having different ends, engage men differ-
ently. He who chooses perfection becomes pure. He
who chooses enjoyment misses the true end." ' Here
the supreme importance of renunciation in the development of man's spiritual life is emphasised. As *Yama* said:
' "That which is beyond never rises before the mind of
a thoughtless child deluded by the folly of riches. This
world exists, the other does not, thinking thus they
come again and again under my power." '

36.2 THE TRUE MEANING OF FAITH

Next Yama says that to know the truth man must
first have faith, and not merely argue about it: 'Many,
even hearing it continually, do not understand it, for
the speaker must be wonderful, so must be the hearer.
The teacher must be wonderful, so must be the taught.
Neither is the mind to be disturbed by vain arguments.
...' The real meaning of faith is conveyed in these two
ideas. Faith does not mean simple credulity or blind

acceptance. It means in the first place that matters of spiritual life, even like matters of natural sciences, cannot be understood by mere arguments. People very well understand that sciences are all based on facts observed, and that man, working on them with his rational thoughts, builds up theories. But strangely enough, many today think that in respect of religion and spiritual doctrines, there are no such apprehensible facts but only vain arguments. So we are told that such vain arguments have no place in spiritual life. Spiritual verities like God, the Atman, etc., are within us. Our thoughts have to be analysed and their deepest layers explored. On these facts are the universal doctrines of religions based. But this should not be interpreted to mean that all kinds of dogmas of religion are to be accepted. The great sages from whom spiritual traditions have originated have only the right to tell us that they have analysed their minds and have found these facts, and if we do the same, we shall also arrive at them. But usually those who attack religions have no patience to analyse their minds, and their arguments have therefore no weight.

It is like the agreement of blind men against those with eyes: ' "You are all fools who believe in the sun." ' If one has seen a country and another compels one to say that one has not, still one cannot give up the conviction in the heart of hearts that one has been there.

When we thus see God and the facts of religion in a more intense sense than we see the external world, then nothing will be able to shake our belief. That is the nature of real faith. There are very few who will reject the idea of faith, when faith is interpreted in this light, not as mere blind intellectual assent to a doctrine, but an assent based on experience of the factual nature of the doctrine that one accepts.

The watchword of Vedanta is therefore realisation and not mere intellectual assent to dogmas: 'He has hidden Himself inside the atom, this Ancient One who resides in the inmost recess of every human heart. The sages realised Him through the power of introspection, and got beyond both joy and misery, beyond what we call virtue and vice, beyond good and bad deeds, beyond being and non-being; he who has seen Him has seen the Reality.'

36.3 HEAVENS AND THEIR SIGNIFICANCE

Various religions, without rising to this high level of realisation, place heavens as the goal for their votaries. Heavens are always described in sensuous language, as an extension of all the pleasurable experiences of the world by men in different societies. Indra's heaven described in the Hindu Puranas is like this. The Arabs' heaven is full of beautiful gardens, with rivers flowing and with all means for a pleasurable life. The Norwegians who delighted in hunting and fighting conceived of a heaven which is a tremendous fighting place with Odin presiding. First a boar hunt; then a mutual fight in which warriors slash each other until all are killed; this is followed by the revival of all and a wild carousal and the eating of the boar's roasted flesh. On the next day the boar again revives and the hunt and other occurrences are repeated; so it goes on eternally.

Now the Vedanta holds that all pursuit of pleasure, including what is implied in the conception of heaven, is an urge of the infinite joy that is the basic nature of the spirit within. 'Wherever there is any blessing, blissfulness, or joy, even the joy of the thief in stealing, it is that absolute bliss coming out, only it has become obscured, muddled up, as it were, with all sorts of extraneous conditions, and misunderstood. But to understand that, we have to go through the negation, and then the positive side will begin. We have to give up ignorance and all that is false, and then truth will begin to reveal itself to us. When we have grasped the truth, things which we gave up at first will take new shape and form, will appear to us in a new light, and become deified. They will have become sublimated, and then we shall understand them in their true light.'

36.4 REALISATION AND THE NATURE OF MAN

Yama then gives a direct answer to the question what happens to men after death. He says: ' "This Wise One never dies, is never born, It arises from nothing, and nothing arises from It. Unborn, Eternal, Everlasting, this Ancient One can never be destroyed with the destruction of the body. If the slayer thinks he can slay, or if the slain thinks he is slain, they both do not know the truth, for the Self neither slays nor is slain." ' The use of the word 'Wise One' is significant. The Atman, the spiritual essence, is the same in all. The wise one is one who is aware of it, and in whose life that spiritual perfection is expressed in a powerful way. In the good and the great it is expressed more; in the ordinary man and in the sinner, its expression is inhibited for want of the awareness of that higher nature by the obstruction of the body and mind and the individual's identification with them. The recognition of one's Atman nature is realisation; its non-recognition is the life of ignorance.

' "This Atman is not to be realised by the power of speech, nor by a vast intellect, nor by the study of their Vedas." ' Then how is it to be realised? It is answered, ' "With whom the Lord is pleased, to that man He expresses Himself." ' But then the objection will be raised that this is something like partisanship. But *Yama* answers: ' "Those who are evil-doers, whose minds are a

not peaceful, can never see the Light. It is to those who
are true in heart, pure in deed, whose senses are controlled, that this Self manifests Itself.' Man is compared
to a rider in the chariot of the body, with intellect as the
driver and the senses as the horses. As the chariot will
not reach the goal unless the horses are properly controlled and directed, man too will fail to reach the spiritual goal if the senses are not brought under control.
'This Atman in all beings does not manifest Himself
to the eyes or the senses, but those whose minds have
become purified and refined realise Him. Beyond all
sound, all sight, beyond form, absolute, beyond all taste
and touch, infinite, without beginning and without end,
even beyond nature, the Unchangeable; he who realises
Him, frees himself from the jaws of death. '

36.5 THE QUESTION OF UTILITY

What is the utility of realisation, and are there not
other alternative ideals? (1) The sense of utility varies
from man to man. It may be that the majority of men
consider sense enjoyment as the most useful. They have
no right to think that all others are constituted the same
way as themselves. There are many who do not think life
worth living for a little gold or some sense enjoyments.
For them spiritual realisation is the only matter of utility. (2) The advocates of sense enjoyment put their case

in a more veiled and apparently noble form. If we go on improving the life of the world, a time will come when all undesirable features of it are eliminated and only the attractive ones will remain. This is a false assessment. The world's misdeeds are like chronic rheumatism. If it is removed from one place, it appears elsewhere. Enjoyments and sufferings have been more or less constant in world history. They have only changed in their appearances, not in the total quantum. Desire is the cause of all misery. And our idea of progress only means increasing our desire. Hence our so-called progress only adds to the world's miseries. (3) There are still others who say that in the world process the Infinite is trying to express itself through the finite, and that a time will come when this will succeed. This too is a fallacious idea. By the nature of things the Infinite cannot be fully manifest in the finite. It can only come about by the finite ceasing to be finite and relapsing into the Infinite. This brings us to the philosophy of renunciation and realisation. For renunciation is the reaction that comes when the limited life, the life of bondage by the senses, becomes unsatisfactory and unbearable; this renunciation is the prelude to realisation.

37

UNITY IN DIVERSITY

37.1 THE FINITE CANNOT EXPRESS THE INFINITE

As among all early religious texts, in the *Vedas* too the quest for reality takes an external direction. But the Vedic thinkers came to understand very soon that the secret of reality is not to be found in the external world but only by looking inwards. For, if the reality we are after is the Infinite, it can never be found in the diversities of the external world, which are all of a finite nature. The Infinite can never be found as expressing itself fully in the finite external objects. The Infinite must be sought only in that which is Infinite, and the only thing Infinite about us is that which is within us, our own innermost soul. This innermost Being is the seer and to Him belongs the body, mind and all the objects of perception. To seek the Infinite cause of the whole universe, we have to go there. To start with, man sought Him above in the skies or in a heaven to be reached hereafter. But the very idea of the Infinite located in space will be a contradiction. It came to be understood that the devas in the heavens too are only finite beings on the path of their evolution. Indra, Varuna and other names of devas indicate certain positions which *jivas* attain to at certain stages of evolution. All these regions and their denizens are subject to the limitation of space and time, and are within the frame-work of the same laws that moulded them into different forms and would crush them out again. So to seek the Infinite basis of everything, we have to go inward and not outward.

37.2 THE WORLD A MIXTURE OF GOOD AND EVIL

The external world is the field of the play of the pairs of opposite forces. Life and death, happiness and misery, good and evil go together. The utilitarian's and the evolutionist's idea that there will be a time when good alone will prevail without any evil, is a vain hope, as it is against the nature of things. People who hold such views think that there is a fixed quantity of good and evil, and that by eliminating the one, the other can be made to prevail exclusively. But the world's history disproves it. It looks that neither of these can be eliminated. With the elimination of certain physical hardships and sufferings, mental ailments and sufferings come in their place, and with the increase of refinement, sensitivity to pain also increases. According to the Vedanta the truth is that good and evil, enjoyment and suffering are not two entirely different entities or two separate essences, but one and the same thing appearing in different degrees and in different guises and producing differences of feeling in the same mind. So the Vedanta seeks to find the unity behind the external diversities, to find the One existence that appears as different in its manifestation. Behind good and evil stands the Reality that is beyond them both and which manifests as both these also.

37.3 GO BEYOND GOOD AND EVIL

Vedanta is, therefore, neither optimistic nor pessimistic. It does not believe that life can be made all enjoyable or all miserable. The quantum of these may increase or decrease under different situations, but will never get eliminated substantially. Vedanta, however, maintains that we can go beyond them both, and then eliminate evil along with the good also, by going to the level of our innermost Self, where we are in the sphere of Infinity unaffected by the opposites of dualistic manifestations. Even this weak mind, which runs after the manifold, can be made strong and made to catch a glimpse of that oneness, which saves one from birth and death. As the rain falling upon a mountain flows in various streams down the sides of the mountain, so all the energies which we see here are from that one unity. It has become manifold falling upon maya. Do not go after the manifold, go towards the one.

" 'He is in all that moves; He is in all that is pure; He fills the universe; He is in the sacrifice; He is in the guest of the house; He is in man, in water, in animals, in truth; He is the Great One. As fire coming into this world is manifesting itself in various forms, even so, that one Soul of the universe manifests itself in various forms, even so, the One Soul of all souls, of all beings, is manifesting Himself in all forms." This is true for you when you have understood this Unity, and not before. Then it is all optimism, because He is seen everywhere.'

37.4 THE UNIVERSAL SPIRIT IS NOT AFFECTED BY EVIL

Then the question will be asked: If the pure and perfect Self has entered into everything, why is there suffering and evil in the world? The only experiencer must be He only, and the question therefore arises, why should the perfect one suffer? The answer of the *Upanishads* is that He does not suffer. Suffering is only an appearance; just as all things appear yellow to a man having jaundice. ' "As the sun is the cause of the eyesight of every being, yet is not made defective by the defect in any eye, even so the Self of all is not affected by the miseries of the body, or by any misery that is around you." '

37.5 DISCOVERY OF
THE SELF—THE MEANS TO PEACE

He who in this world of evanescence finds Him who never changes, he who in this universe of death finds that one life, he who in this manifold finds that oneness, and all those who realise Him as the soul of their souls—to them belongs eternal peace, unto none else. But He cannot be found in the external world—in the sun or stars. He is the ultimate subject, and can therefore be experienced only on the side of the subject that is within. Or, He is like a banyan tree spreading everywhere, with all branches and leaves interconnected and having their source ultimately in the root, which is He. He is not to be known in heavens. In different heavens He is experienced hazily as we see things in dream, or as one sees one's own reflection in water, or at the most as light and shade as in *brahmaloka*. But as a man sees his own face in a mirror, perfect, distinct and clear, so is the truth shining in the soul of man. The highest heaven is therefore in our own souls. If we die and go to heaven, or even while living, go to a cave or a forest or a holy place, we get no vision of Him unless we carry the polished mirror of a pure heart; and with that mirror we can get at the reality as it is, irrespective of where we are. When all the vain desires of the heart are given up, when all the knots of the heart are cut asunder, then this very mortal becomes immortal, thus he becomes one with God even here.

37.6 PRACTICALITY OF VEDANTA

Sometimes these ideals of Vedanta are decried as the impracticality and other-worldliness of the easterner. But the fact is that Indian philosophers deprecate the idea of going to heaven, and exhort man to achieve the highest here in this world itself. Salvation is to be had here according to the Vedanta, and for this the other-worldliness has to be got over. The Hindu is as practical as the westerner, only his view of life is different from what is inculcated in the west. An American material-istic philosopher spoke of an ideal life as a full life here on earth, and compared it to squeezing an orange dry. But the Hindu too thinks that this fruit of life should be squeezed, but he prefers a mango to an orange. The man in the west thinks that to eat and drink and have a little scientific knowledge is what is expected of us in life. But he cannot contend that this is the only worthy way of living. Some may consider this a very unworthy way of life. The Hindu wants to understand the heart of things, the very kernel itself. The study of the west is concerned with the manifestation of life, but the Indian philosopher's is life itself. He wants to know the 'why' of things, and leaves the 'how' to children. It is good and great to be scientific but when a person thinks that it is all that matters, he is talking foolishly; for he is neglecting the raison d'etre of life by not studying existence itself. So both these types of men are practical, but their mistake lies in regarding this world as the whole of life. Practicality there is in the scientific field, and there is practicality in the spiritual field too. A combination of both these will pave the way for a better world in the harmony of oneness.

38

THE FREEDOM OF THE SOUL

38.1 EVOLUTION OF VEDANTIC
LITERATURE AND THOUGHT

In the later *Upanishads* like the *Katha*, all the spiritual ideas have been brought together into one place. It is still more conspicuously so in the case of the *Bhagavad Gita* which is probably the last of the *Upanishads*. In the Vedantic writings of this type, we cannot find sufficient data to trace the development of thought. But in the older *Upanishads* like the *Chandogya* we find traces of the gradual evolution of Vedic religion from ritualism to meditation and from that to spirituality.

The trend of thought is this: the multiplicity of gods gives place to the one God of the universe. Even when the many gods are retained, there is a tendency to look upon them as the manifestations of the one God. But it did not stop with this. The one all powerful personal God was also found unsatisfactory, just as the several great nations found the rule by one all-powerful king intolerable and discovered an ideal government in an impersonal system, which has come to be called democracy in modern times. At the climax of thought the personality of God vanishes and impersonality comes in. God is no more a person, no more a human being, however magnified and exaggerated, who rules the universe, but He becomes an embodied principle in every being, immanent in the whole universe. It would be illogical to go from the personal God to the impersonal, leaving man as a person. So the personal man also is broken down and man as a principle is built up. The personal man becomes a mere phenomenon, while the principle, the impersonal Man behind becomes the 'reality'. In the next stage of development there is the gradual convergence of the advancing lines of impersonal God and impersonal Man. The *Upanishads* embody the stages through which these two lines at last became one, and the last word of each *Upanishad* is 'Thou art That.' There is but one eternally blissful principle, and that One is manifesting as all the variety.

With this the Upanishadic sages stop and then the threads of their thought are taken up by philosophers who fill in the details and give logical consistency to the teachings as a system of thought. The one question that is raised always about a non-dual theory of existence is, how the One became the many. Why does evil exist in a world that is attributed to a perfect Being? 'the best answer that India has produced is the theory of Maya

which says that It really has not become manifold, that
It really has not lost any of Its real nature. Manifoldness
is only apparent. Man is only apparently a person, but
in reality he is the Impersonal Being. God is a person
only apparently, but really He is the Impersonal Being.'

All philosophers, however, did not accept the maya
theory, and therefore there came into existence various other interpretations.of the Upanishadic thought
by dualistic and quasi-dualistic thinkers. Pure dualists
think man has no right to ask the question why the perfect produced this imperfect world. The will of God is
satisfactory for them as reason for everything. God has
pre-destined the fate of souls, and man has to accept it
with resignation. They support their ideas with Vedic
texts interpreted by them in their own way. There are
the quasi-monists who stand midway, accepting a kind
of unity without the maya theory. According to them
the whole of this creation forms, as it were, the body
of God inseparable from Him. God is the Soul of all
souls and of nature.

38.2 THE DOCTRINE OF THE DIVINITY OF MAN

Through all these systems of thoughts there is one
idea running, and that is the divinity of man, that the
soul of man is essentially pure and perfect. In fact all
religions admit this in a mythological fashion. The pure

dualistic idea is that of a God and a devil, an Ahura and an Ahriman. Originally created pure, man degenerates and becomes a sinner by succumbing to the seduction of the devil, and he can be saved and restored to his pristine state by God's grace only. Hindu dualists will attribute the bondage of the *jiva* to the load of karma. When suffering comes, it is to be endured patiently; if this is not done, one will be punished all the more. There is no liberty for the human soul, and some are predestined to spiritual degradation. Omnipotence of God is accepted, and no 'why' can therefore be asked about His ways. Then there are others who are qualified monists who hold a *via media* theory regarding God and man's destiny, in the place of the maya theory which denies the actuality of the degradation of the spirit. They say that the whole of creation, including the world and all the *jivas*, forms, as it were, the body of God. God is the soul of all souls and of all nature. The spiritual consciousness of *jivas* gets contracted by evil action, and good work leads to its greater and greater manifestation. The inherent spiritual nature of the *jivas* cannot be obliterated in any way.

Most of these religions either through the language of mythology or philosophy, maintain that originally the spirit in man was pure, and the evil nature of it is of a passing nature, brought about by transgression. Some systems may make God and the devil into two entities, others may make them both into one, and a third may totally deny the actuality of evil. Out of all these superstitions and speculations, the one idea that comes out is 'that man is divine, that divinity is our nature.'

The Vedanta would say that the evil that seems to have affected the soul is only a superimposition, which means that the soul's pristine purity has never been effaced even when it appeared to be degraded. Purity is not a quality of the soul but its very nature. A quality is something that was not there but which came to be acquired, and which can, for the same reason, be lost also. What is natural cannot be lost. It may be hidden, but it is never lost. It is like a flint which may be moist in water, but friction will bring out the fire from it; this quality of it can never be effaced, because it is of its essence. The difference between the *Maya-vadin* and the others may be thus stated. The others say we had a great empire, we have lost it, and have to try to get it back. But the *Maya-vadin* contends that this losing of the empire is a hallucination. You never lost it. You are always that, for your essential nature can never be lost, though it may be hidden.

Now hidden or lost, how is the empire to be recovered? Dualistic religions give various answers: by certain ceremonies; by making some offering to deities or priests; by eating particular foods and living in particular ways; by weeping, prostrating and seeking par-

don of some Being beyond nature; by loving that Being
with all one's heart and so on. 'All this varied advice
is in the Upanishads. ... But the last and the greatest
counsel is that you need not weep at all. You need not
go through all these ceremonies, and need not take any
notice of how to regain your empire, because you never
lost it. Why should you go to seek for what you never
lost? You are pure already, you are free already. If you
think you are free, free you are this moment, and if you
think you are bound, bound you will be. This is a very
bold statement, and as I told you at the beginning of
this course, I shall have to speak to you very boldly. It
may frighten you now, but when you think over it, and
realise it in your own life, then you will come to know
that what I say is true. For, supposing that freedom is
not your nature, by no manner of means can you become free. Supposing you were free and in some way
you lost that freedom, that shows that you were not
free to begin with. Had you been free, what could have
made you lose it? The independent can never be made
dependent; if it is really dependent, its independence
was a hallucination. ... So if it is possible for us to attain to freedom, the conclusion is inevitable that the
soul is by its nature free. ... Of these two which will
you take? Either make the first a delusion, or make the
second a delusion. Certainly I will make the second a
delusion. It is more consonant with all my feelings and

aspirations. I am perfectly aware that I am free by nature, and I will not admit that this bondage is true and
my freedom a delusion.'

38.3 SPIRITUALISM VERSUS MATERIALISM

This line of thought is applicable also to the problem
of relation between matter and consciousness. Meteri-
alistic philosophers say that there is no soul, or a conscious entity apart from the body. What is called the
soul is only a delusion produced by the repeated transit
of particles of matter bringing about the combination
which is called the brain; the impression of freedom is
the result of the vibration and motion and continuous
transit of these particles. There were Buddhist sects
also who illustrated this with the example of a rapidly
circling torch giving the delusive idea of a continuous
circle. The spiritualists reverse the argument and say
that it is thought that projects matter as its object by
virtue of its rapid motion, and the notion of reality of
matter is a delusion. The arguments on both sides are
similar; only those on the spiritualists' side seem to be
in a stronger position. For, nobody has ever seen what
matter is in itself. We can only feel ourselves; for, when
we call a thing as existing outside, we are only giving
an interpretation of sensations felt within ourselves. No
one can jump out of himself and experience matter as

such. Besides, the spirit theory explains the universe, while materialism does not at all do so.

38.4 ADVAITISM AS THE SAVING GOSPEL FOR MAN

The Advaitin's solution of the riddle of the soul's bondage is the uncompromising assertion that the Atman was never bound, but is ever free. Even to say that we are now bound and that we shall attain to freedom by various sadhanas is dangerous, because it is a kind of self- hypnotism even to admit that the Atman is in bondage in any sense. The pure Advaitin's sadhana does not consist in admitting bondage and then getting rid of it, which is un-psychological. He straightway asserts his perpetual Selfhood, and unhesitatingly and uncompromisingly declares 'Sivoham'—'I am He, I am He' There are no doubt very noble and attractive ideas in dualistic thought which accepts a personal God apart from nature. These ideas may be very soothing. 'But, says the Vedanta, the soothing is something like the effect that comes from an opiate, not natural. It brings weakness in the long run, and what this world wants today, more than it ever did before, is strength. ... Weakness is the one cause of suffering. ... We lie, steal, kill, and commit other crimes, because we are weak. We suffer because we are weak. We die because we are weak. Where there is nothing to weaken us, there is no

death nor sorrow. We are miserable through delusion.
Give up the delusion, and the whole thing vanishes. ...
Through all these philosophical discussions and tremendous mental gymnastics we come to this one religious
idea, the simplest in the whole world.'

38.5 THE QUESTION OF THE
PRACTICALITY OF ADVAITISM

To teach dualism was a tremendous mistake made
in India and elsewhere. The Advaita was reserved for
sannyasins, and the generality of men were taught only
dualistic religious thoughts. This is largely due to two
mistaken notions about Advaita; (a) that Advaitism is
too difficult for ordinary man; and (b) that the public
preaching of such a philosophy will lead to moral laxity. Both these ideas are wrong. That it is the simplest
doctrine has already been shown. It may be that the
philosophical and logical processes by which it is arrived at are complicated, but its principle is very simple.
That principle consists in understanding and asserting
the idea that the spirit in man is divine and has never
been affected by impurity or bondage. And as for the
contention that the preaching of it will lead to laxity and
immorality, it is a shallow and thoughtless criticism. On
the contrary, it is the only antidote to such perversities
in men. Every sinful tendency is a form of weakness,

and weakness cannot be effaced by repeatedly suggesting that we are weak. It can be effaced only by asserting the basic purity and divinity of the human spirit. In place of doing this, many of the dualistic doctrines seek to fill man's mind with superstition and a sense of dependence on extraneous entities. Some cannot think of being religious without accepting a devil and the whimsical and autocratic rule of a personal God sitting in a far off heaven. In place of filling the mind with all such superstitions which weaken man and put him into a state of stupor as by an opiate, let him listen to the truth about his real nature, the divinity of the spirit, which is the message that Advaita conveys to him. He will then be established in strength, freed from corruptions and made self-reliant. When there is no devil and no personal God outside to throw the responsibility for one's actions upon, man will become self-reliant, strong, self-respecting—in every sense a better man morally and spiritually.

Dualistic ideas have ruled the world long enough and the results are not very encouraging. Why not then make a new experiment by teaching the religion of Advaitism to everyone, instead of confining it to *sannyasins* alone as in the past? It may be said that even if this ideal is accepted, it is difficult in practice. Merely to say with one's lips, ' "I am the Pure, the Blessed' ", may be easy, but one cannot be that always in life. But would 'it mend matters to go towards superstition? If we cannot get nectar, would it mend matters for us to drink poison? Would it be of any help for us, because we cannot realise the truth immediately, to go into darkness and yield to weakness and superstition?

'I have no objection to dualism in many of its forms. I like most of them, but I have objections to every form of teaching which inculcates weakness. ... I know that truth alone gives life, and nothing but going towards reality will make us strong, and none will reach truth until he is strong. ... Nothing makes us so moral as this idea of monism. Nothing makes us work so well at our best and highest as when all the responsibility is thrown upon ourselves.

"I have neither death nor fear, I have neither caste nor creed, I have neither father nor mother nor brother, neither friend nor foe, for I am Existence, Knowledge, and Bliss Absolute; I am the Blissful One, I am the Blissful One. ... I have neither hunger nor thirst; the body is not mine, nor am I subject to the superstitions and decay that come to the body, I am Existence, Knowledge, and Bliss Absolute; I am the Blissful One, I am the Blissful One." ' This, says the Vedantist, is the only prayer we should have.

39

THE COSMOS—THE MACROCOSM

The power and beauty of nature has always impressed the human mind ever since it got the power of reflection, and the question has been asked: What is this universe and where has it come from? In the *Vedas*, the most ancient literature, the question is thus put: ' "Whence is this? When there was neither aught nor naught, and darkness was hidden in darkness, who projected this universe? How? Who knows the secret?' " But is this assumption behind the question that there was a time when the worlds did not exist at all—is it correct? Are we sure of it? If it is interpreted to mean that there was an absolute beginning for the world, it is an un-philosophical position. An examination of nature's processes will show that the beginning of an entity means only the re-emergence of it from the causal condition into which it had been dissolved earlier. From a small seed a big tree gradually comes up and again ends in small seeds in which the power of the tree is held latent or unmanifest. Under propitious conditions the tree comes out of it again. Out of an egg a bird comes up, or out of a seminal cell, an animal or a man comes up. Again they relapse into the seminal condition, from which they emerge in course of time. A rain drop was drawn from the sea as vapour to form the cloud, and when it rains, it comes back as the drop of water. Huge mountains are in the course of ages washed down as fine dust by rain into the sea where under pressure of water they again become rocks to be thrown up as mountains by geophysical forces working within the bowels of the earth. Thus everything in nature begins, as it were, from certain seeds, certain rudiments, certain fine forms, and becomes grosser and grosser, and develops, going on that way for a certain time, and then again goes back to that fine form and subsides, only to come out again in the same form in course of time. If nature's processes are uniform, this law of cyclic mani-festation must be applicable to the universe as a whole. The manifested universe must dissolve back into the nebulous state from which it had come out, and it should come out of it again in the process of time.

39.2 THE IMPLICATIONS OF THE CYCLIC PROCESS

If we observe this cosmic process, we find that there are three principles involved in it: (1) The effect is not different from the cause. It is only a reproduction of the cause in a gross form. The cause is the fine condition; and when the same entity assumes the gross condition, it becomes the effect. (2) The process is cyclic. There is no absolute beginning, and nothing entirely new is produced. What existed once in a gross form, goes back to its fine causal condition, and again comes into the former gross condition. What is called the beginning is only a re-emergence in a cyclic process. There is no creation out of nothing. (3) Between two gross manifestations, there is an intervening period of inactivity. A seed does not become a tree immediately. There is a period of inactivity in the soil until conditions of heat and moisture become propitious. Then activities start, and the slow process ends with the manifestation of the big tree. So also the universe in the process of time dissolves into the elements and finally into the subtle and unmanifested seminal condition. Then it is in an abeyant state for a time, which is called *pralaya* or dissolution, at the end of which the process of re-emergence starts. This whole period of manifestation, abeyance and re-emergence is called a *kalpa* or cosmic cycle, which the cosmologists of the *Puranas* calculate in millions and millions of years.

39.3 SPIRITUAL THEORY OF EVOLUTION

The cyclic theory of creation also implies a spiritual conception of evolution. Logically speaking, evolution presupposes an involution. For, according to the laws of physics, we can get out of a machine only the same quantum of energy which we have put into it in another form. The energy of coal and water or of oil that is put in a vehicle is what comes out as the motion of the vehicle. Corresponding to this fuelling of the machine, there is in the cosmic process an involution of the energies, form, intelligence, etc., and it is only this that makes the process of evolution of a new world of life and intelligence possible. The modern theory of evolution knows nothing of this process of involution, and it has to be supplemented by the Indian idea of the cyclic process of nature.

The cyclic theory also presupposes the precedence of spirit over matter, of God over creation. In the modern theory of evolution, a protoplasm develops into a Buddha or a Christ, and logically the intelligence that represents these great personalities must have been involved in the protoplasm at the very beginning of evolution. According to the modern theory, however, it is only after millennia of material evolution, that intelligence appeared in that particular formation called brain matter. But this theory is an imperfect and truncated one, and fails to explain evolution or make it intelligible. Not only in the case of the individual, but in the case of the whole universe, the involution of intelligence has to be accepted, in order to explain the sum-total of intelligence that unfolds itself in the course of evolution. This universal intelligence that provides the urge and direction for evolution is what is called God. Call it by any other name, it is absolutely certain that in the beginning, there is that infinite cosmic intelligence. It gets involved, and then it manifests, evolves itself until it becomes the perfect man, the Christ-man or the Buddha-man, and goes back to its pristine condition. That is why the scriptures teach that we come from God and go back to God.

Thus we see that all the various forms of cosmic energy such as matter, thought-force, intelligence and so on are simply the manifestations of the cosmic intelligence, or as He is familiarly called, the Supreme Lord. 'Everything that you see, feel, or hear, the whole universe, is His creation, or to be a little more accurate, is His projection; or to be still more accurate, is the Lord Himself. ... He Himself is both the material and the efficient cause of this universe, and He it is that gets involved in the minute cell, and evolves at the other end and becomes God again. He it is that comes down and becomes the lowest atom, and slowly unfolding His nature, rejoins Himself. This is the mystery of the universe.'

40

THE COSMOS—THE MICROCOSM

40.1 HOW PERCEPTION TAKES PLACE

Man's quest for Truth in his primitive condition was largely directed towards external nature, and he filled all natural phenomena and even objects of every day experience like rivers, trees and mountains with spirits and gods controlling them. At a more mature stage of thought he found that the quest outside took him nowhere, and that it would be more rewarding to study his own nature, the internal man.

At some time in their life the question is asked by all men, the wise as well as the ignorant, the rich as well as the poor—whether there is anything enduring in this evanescent human life, whether there is anything in us which does not perish with the body. The question was answered thousands of years back by the thinkers of the *Upanishads*, and their analysis of the inner man is to the following effect:

We have to go from the external physical man to his innermost core, step by step. We perceive things. Take sight for example. For sight, we first of all require the physical eye, without which sight is impossible. But it is not sufficient. Behind it is the organ, the nerve centre in the brain, to enable the physical eye to see things. But even if vibrations of light reach the nerve centre, sight will not take place if the mind is not attached to it, say, as in the absence of visual perception when we are intently hearing something. Mind too is only a carrier, it has to present the impression to the intellect which determines the nature of the impression by comparing it with earlier impressions. Even the awareness of the object can arise only when the intellect presents the impression to the self-conscious principle in man, the spiritual essence in him, which in popular language is called the soul of man. Up to the intellect, all parts in man are material, may be of increasingly subtler aspects of nature, and are without the revealing light of consciousness in them. What is seen in these as consciousness is only the borrowed or reflected light of the Atman.

40.2 THE SELF-CONSCIOUS PRINCIPLE IN MAN

In these different layers of the personality of man, the grossest part, which we call the physical body, is perishable within a short period. The fine layer or the body constituted of the mind and intellect is not so easily perishable, though it may degenerate in its functioning when the physical body, through which it expresses and functions, is affected by lack of nourishment or old age. Since the subtle mental layer is found to degenerate, it is also like the physical body, an aspect of matter and we have to go deeper than the mind for the self-conscious and undecaying spiritual essence in man.

How can we know that there is something behind mind? Because, it is an absolute necessity of thought and experience to accept such a self-conscious entity behind it. Matter in itself is not conscious. Earth, metals, timber and other material substances are not aware of anything outside or of themselves. But the material substance in our organism, the body, is conscious of external things, and is also aware that it is oneself that is conscious of them, *i.e.,* it is both conscious and self-conscious. But these faculties of the body are temporary and can wax and wane according to its condition. At death the body loses these faculties completely. We have therefore to conclude that these powers of self-consciousness and other-consciousness of the body must be a borrowed faculty only. It cannot be attributed to the mind also, because though we experience that it is the presence of the mind that makes us self-conscious, reflection shows us that the position of the mind too is exactly like that of the body. Its powers increase and decrease, but that which is self-luminous by nature, or rather self-luminosity itself, cannot decay. It is only the luminosity of that which shines through a borrowed light that comes and goes, and not of that which is in itself pure self-luminosity. So the mind also is not self-luminous, and we have therefore got to accept behind the mind a pure self-luminous principle, which is ever aware of itself and makes the consciousness of everything else also possible—which, through its association, lends its luminosity to inert material entities like the mind, senses and the body, and makes them self-conscious for the time being, just as fire makes an iron ball red hot for a time. This is the ruler of the body and the mind, the soul of man, the king on the throne, by whose association the mind and body become capable of self-conscious apprehension.

This self-consciousness cannot be explained as an end-product of a material process, as materialists would like to do. The chain of cause and effects may be traced from the external object to the physical, nervous and brain stimulations, but the 'I-sense' which illumines the whole process with a sense of awareness is so different in quality from all the earlier mechanical processes, that we cannot call it an end-product at all. It has to be accounted for as the inflow of a totally non-physical spiritual energy, the light of Self-consciousness, the unique characteristic of which is the awareness of an object accompanied with the sense, I am aware of it. This self-illuminating intelligence cannot belong to the dull dead matter. Self-luminosity indicates the presence of an entity whose essence is intelligence—the Atman or the spiritual principle in man, which does not die with the body.

40.3 THE DOCTRINE OF RE-BIRTH

The existence of the soul is to be understood from its self-luminosity. Knowledge, blessedness, and existence form its essence unlike objects without self-luminosity. It has been eternally existent and never created. As non-created, it is not limited by time. Time is within it. It has neither birth nor death, but being in association with material insentient vehicles, it is manifesting slowly and gradually from lower to higher expressions. It is expressing its own grandeur, working through the mind and the body. Through the body it is grasping the external world and understanding it. It takes up a body and uses it, and when that body has failed and is used up, it takes another body, and so on it goes.

This brings us to the question of the re-birth or re-incarnation of the soul. The followers of certain religions conceive that they did not even in essence exist at one time, that they came out of zero, a nothing, but they will none-the-less continue to exist through eternity. Now the theory of reincarnation tells man, in the predicament in which he finds himself, that he has been eternally existing, that for this reason he will never become a zero, and that his appearance in a body is meant for the gradual emergence of his spiritual potentialities as the Atman, and that these embodiments are meant for him to gather experience and gain wisdom, and will end when he has realised his nature as the ever-blissful Atman unaffected by any change.

Although this is by far the most satisfactory explanation of man from a spiritual and rational stand-point, it has been objected to by critics, especially by those who uphold the doctrine of the soul being created in time, on the ground that we do not remember the past. The presumption here is that memory is the proof of our past experiences. This argument is manifestly absurd, because many of the occurrences of our past, especially of infancy and childhood, are not remembered at all.

Again the assumption is wrong factually also. The memory of all the past births does come to a man in his last birth, at the moment he attains knowledge and liberation. 'then the mind will see dearly as daylight how many times all these existed for you, how many millions of times you had fathers and mothers, sons and daughters, husbands and wives, relatives and friends, wealth and power. They came and went. How many times you were on the topmost crest of the wave, and how many times you were down at the bottom of despair! When memory will bring all these to you, then alone will you

stand as a hero and smile when the world frowns upon
you. Then alone will you stand up and say, "I care not
for thee even, O Death; what terrors hast thou for me?"
    This will come to all.

40.4 PROOFS OF PAST BIRTH

As for the rationale of the theory, it alone accounts
for the wide divergence between man and man in the
power to acquire knowledge. A piece of new knowledge
is not a solitary phenomenon, but the result of a collective process, which may be described as pigeon-holing
experience. Man has a fund of experiences classified
and arranged, as it were, and when a new experience
comes, it is pigeon-holed into these pockets of mental
impression, and by comparison with their contents, it is
recognised as such and such. If a child comes into the
world with what is called a *tabula rasa,* a mind without
any impression, such a child can gain no intellectual
advancement, because there is no background with
which to compare experiences and gain understanding.
There are differences in the power of acquiring knowledge between individuals, because each one has come
with his own fund of knowledge and not with a blank
or uniform mind.

Next take the presence of instinctive wisdom in birds,
animals and men. A bird building its complicated nest,

a duckling rushing into water, creatures even from infancy showing signs of fear of death and so many other forms of behaviour based on untaught wisdom—these can be accounted for only by assuming that all these creatures had repealed experiences, which have made these peculiar patterns of behaviour automatic with them. Experience is the only way by which knowledge is gained, and it is repeated experience that would help one do anything without thought or effort. Death for example is universally feared by all creatures. Unless death were experienced countless times before, how could the automatic fear of it exist? There is also the phenomenon that there are many muscles in the body that are now working automatically without any conscious control. But by proper efforts and exercises all of them can be regulated and brought under control, under the direction of the will. What could thus be undone by effort, must have been acquired also by effort if not in this life, then in lives past. Thus without taking the past into account, the present behaviour and further intellectual development of beings cannot be explained.

40.5 THEORY OF HEREDITY: AN INADEQUATE EXPLANATION

An alternative explanation for all this from the point of view of materialism is offered by certain thinkers in the theory of hereditary transmission. This theory can be accepted partly, that is, as far as supplying the physical material for the manifestation of the re-incarnating mind is concerned. A soul by its past actions accumulates impressions only through a particular physical vehicle. By the moral force of karma (actions of the past), that soul automatically goes for embodiment to parents who can provide the physical heredity suited for the display of that soul's potentialities.

Without accepting such a spiritual basis, pure heredity offers no satisfactory explanation of the mental equipment with which new individuals come into the world. The theory of heredity is that the impressions registered in the germ cell are transferred from generation to generation, as there is continuity in the germ cell. Thus in the bioplasmic cell, the limitless impressions of all time are compressed and transmitted to the offspring. Now this is a dogmatic position. It is impossible to understand how this compression of all mental impressions is done in a tiny germ cell. Until these biologists can prove how and where those impressions live in the cell, and what they mean by mental impressions sleeping in the physical cell, their position cannot be taken for granted. It is simpler and more understandable to hold that pure bodily tendencies alone are transmitted through the germ cell, that the mental impressions are carried by a psychic medium which transmigrates and which takes a rebirth through a body that can provide it with the germ cell that can develop a physical vehicle required for the display, in physical life, of the mental and moral efficiencies it is bringing with itself from the past. The theory then comes to this, that there is heredity transmission so far as furnishing the materials to the soul for embodiment is concerned. But the soul migrates and manufactures body after body, and each thought we think, each deed we do, is stored as moral efficiency in the soul, ready to spring up again and take shape at the proper time. The sum-total of these impressions gives the soul the direction for the next birth, when the body it utilised till then perishes. If these impressions are such that they have to manufacture a new body for further experience, the soul will go to those parents who are ready to supply it with suitable material for that body. Thus from body to body it will go, sometimes to heavens and back again to earth, becoming a man, or even sometimes a lower animal if its previous life were unrestrained, immoral and sinful in the extreme. This way it will go on till it has finished its experience and completed the circle. It then knows its own nature, knows what it is, and when ignorance vanishes, its powers become manifest. It becomes perfect, and there is no more necessity to work through physical bodies or through finer mental bodies. It shines in its own light, and is free, no more to be born or to die.

41

IMMORTALITY

41.1 REINCARNATION AND HUMAN FREEDOM

This theory of human personality has another advantage over others. It is the only theory that advocates the freedom of the human soul, and discourages the human tendency to lay all the blame for our weaknesses and sufferings on someone else or on a God or on a conjured-up ghost called fate. What is fate? It is only what we have made ourselves into. We are the makers of our own fate, we reap what we sow. None else has the blame, none else the praise. 'The wind is blowing; those vessels whose sails are unfurled catch it, and go forward on their way, but those which have their sails furled do not catch the wind. Is that the fault of the wind? Is it the fault of the merciful Father, whose wind of mercy is blowing without ceasing, day and night, whose mercy knows no decay, is it His fault that some of us are happy and some unhappy? We make our own destiny. His sun shines for the weak as well as for the strong. His wind blows for saint and sinner alike. He is the Lord of all, the Father of all, merciful, and impartial. ... Our attempts to lay the blame on Him, making Him the punisher, and the rewarder, are only foolish. He neither punishes, nor rewards any. His infinite mercy is open to every one, at all times, in all places, under all conditions, unfailing, unswerving. Upon *us* depends how we use it. Upon us depends how we utilise it. Blame neither man, nor God, nor anyone in the world. When you find yourselves suffering, blame yourselves, and try to do better.'

41.2 *JIVA'S* IMMORTALITY
AS PART OF THE COSMIC MIND

The question of the immortality of the human soul has been one of perennial interest for man. Philosophers, kings, priests, commoners—all have discussed it or thought over it, enquiring whether there is an immortal element in the perishable personality of man. Some have given up the quest as insoluble, and advised people to concern themselves exclusively with the affairs of our physical life. In the turmoil and struggle of life, people may sometimes follow this apparently wise advice, but when suddenly someone whom they love passes away, the old question comes to them again—what after this? What becomes of the soul?

Observing life around, we find it is an eternally recurring cyclic process. The plant or the tree springs from a seed, and before it perishes, leaves its potentialities in another generation of seeds, from which trees come out again. Animals and men are born of tiny germ cells, and they die after a time, leaving progeny with the same capacity to produce germ cells that could give birth to new individuals with all the characteristics of the species. Mountains crumble into dust to become again mountains in the course of the following geological ages. Water from the seas goes up as vapour to come back again as rain. There are two aspects to this cyclic process in nature, to one of which alone modern thought has given special stress. We speak of evolution, by which we mean that from primitive causal conditions, more complicated and perfected forms gradually arise through well-marked stages. But experience tells us that an evolution must have been preceded by an involution. If out of the seed the tree evolves, the tree that comes out is not anything entirely new, but what has preceded the seed and perished, leaving its potentialities in the seed. For, only the seed of a particular tree can produce a similar tree and not a grain of sand. The seed is the cause and the tree the effect. The effect was involved in the cause and it is the involved effect that evolves as the tree. Thus evolution presupposes involution. It is only the energy that is put into a machine at one end that comes out as motion at the other. From a zero nothing but a zero can

be got. As of individuals, this law of involution and evolution is true with regard to species and to the universe
as a whole too. If out of primitive protoplasm, all living
species have evolved, bringing out at the other end great
men like the Buddhas and the Christs, that primitive protoplasm must in some way have all that effect involved
in it. The whole of the manifested universe has come out
of a primitive condition in which the potentialities of the
whole universe were involved. This involved potentiality
in the cosmic whole is divine wisdom, the cosmic consciousness or mind, which is identical with what people
call the Lord or God or Christ or Buddha or Brahman.
All *jivas* are parts of that cosmic mind and are in that
sense immortal like the cosmic mind itself.

41.3 WHY MAN AS ATMAN IS IMMORTAL

The question of immortality of the soul has to be
considered from another point of view also. All objects
we see in the world are compounds formed of matter
and force. Being a combination of parts, these parts
are bound to disintegrate and decay in the course of
nature's processes. But the soul is neither matter nor
force. It is not thought even. It is the manufacturer of
thought, but not thought. It is the manufacturer of the
body too, but it is not the body. Body cannot be the
soul, because the body is not intelligent.

It is conscious, only because it is utilised by something behind it to contact the external world. That power behind is the mind. If the mind is not attached to the sensations coming through the sense organs in the body, the body will have no awareness of them. In illustration may be cited the fact that one hears nothing when one is reading something with great interest and attention. But the intelligence of the mind even is borrowed. For we find the powers of the mind wax and wane. Just like the body, it is also a combination of various subtler elements of *prakriti*. There are cases of double personality when one part of the mind and its contents alone are in the field of consciousness and the others shut off. Such a person may speak an unknown language, which he had heard in childhood but has till now been completely out of his memory. If consciousness is only a product of the molecular changes in the brain such a phenomenon cannot be satisfactorily explained. It is more reasonable to explain it by the theory that in these conditions certain aspects or sections of the mental content are exposed to the light of a self-luminous entity that is beyond the mind, while the others are shut off from it.

That self-luminous entity which forms the core of man's personality is the soul. Self-luminosity means that it can reveal itself and reveal others simultaneously and give the awareness that one is experiencing. No mechanical explanation of the process of perception, tracing it from external movements to the innermost, can explain the experience of 'I see', 'I hear' at the final end of the chain of action and reaction, without attributing it to a simultaneously 'self-revealing' and 'other-revealing' entity. This is the spiritual essence, the Atman in man. It is beyond the law of causation, not being the product of anything. For this reason it is not a compound, and it is therefore indestructible also unlike the apparently conscious entities included in the realm of matter (*prakriti*), which are all effects and compounds. Immortality for man is in the self-luminous Atman, the essence in him. It will never die, because death means going back to the component parts, and that which is not a compound and has no component parts, can never die.

41.4 THE TRUE MEANING OF IMMORTALITY

If we accept that the soul has no death, we have also to accept that it has no life too. For life and death are the obverse and the reverse of the same coin. In the absence of the one, the other also cannot be. This enigma is solved when we remember that the soul is not something that originates and ceases to be, but a part of the cosmic energy which is God. As such, it is beyond life and death. Birth and death spoken of in connection with it, relate only to the body with which it is associated. But its connection with the body is not real; it is only a hallucination. It is omnipresent and cannot therefore be limited by the body. A material substance, say, a piece of wood, cannot be omnipresent, because the surrounding matter forces it to take a form and be limited by it. But the soul, the Atman, which is beyond law, and cannot therefore have anything to condition it, must be omnipresent, and all talks of one being born and dying, must be born of ignorance and the hallucination produced by it. These talks are due to the hallucination resulting from identification with the fine body which we call mind. When a train is moving fast, one sitting in it may feel that the scenery before him is moving. The experience of change in the Atman is a delusion like that, the change of the body being falsely attributed to it. There is therefore nothing like birth and therefore no death for the Atman. It is eternal, omnipresent, omniscient and unconditioned, the experience of its birth and death being mere hallucination.

There are countless numbers of beings, and if the Atman in every one of them be unconditioned and omnipresent, there must be countless such beings. This is an impossible and absurd position. The Vedantist, therefore, answers that this is not so, because the assumption that there are several Atmans is wrong. 'there is only one such Self, and that One Self is you. Standing behind this little nature is what we call the soul. There is only One Being, One Existence, the ever-blessed, the omnipresent, the omniscient, the birthless, the deathless. ... "He is the Soul of your soul, nay, more, you are He, you are one with Him". ... As long as you see the many, you are under delusion. ... Know that thou art He; thou art the God of the Universe, "Tat tvam asi"... All these various ideas that I am a man or a woman, or sick or healthy, or strong or weak, or that I hate, or love, or have a little power are but hallucinations.'

'What frightens you, what holds you down? Only ignorance and delusion; nothing else can bind you. You are the Pure One, the Ever-blessed. ... Silly fools tell you that you are sinners, and you sit down in a corner and weep. It is foolishness, wickedness, downright rascality to say that you are sinners! You are all God. See you not God and call Him man? Therefore, if you dare, stand on that—mould your whole life on that.'

42

THE ATMAN

The religious systems of India are divided into two classes—as the unorthodox and the orthodox. By the former is meant the systems that do not recognise the Vedic authority, and the most important systems included in it are the Jaina and the Buddhistic schools. The orthodox systems recognising the *Veda*, can be mainly divided into three—the Samkhya, the Nyaya and the Mimamsà. The former two, though they are studied as pure intellectual systems, have no adherents today, and whatever contributions they have to make to thought, logic and exegesis have been absorbed by the Mimamsa, which means philosophy based on the interpretation and explanation of the Vedic revelation. There are two sections among the Mimamsakas, one concerned with the Vedic ritualism and the other with the philosophy of the Vedas embodied in the *Upanishads*. The followers of the *Upanishads* are called the

Vedantins. This is the only living religious philosophy of India today and this philosophy has absorbed into it all relevant contributions that the other systems have to make to thought and life.

Sometimes people identify Vedanta with one of its schools, the Advaita. This is not correct. The Upanishadic philosophy has various phases, and the Advaita is only the most reputed of them, although in point of adherents it may not equal the other systems. In spite of the great variations in their philosophic teachings, all these Vedantic systems have got several common points of agreement.

The following points of agreement may be cited: (1) They all accept the *Veda* as the revealed word of God. Their idea is that the *Vedas* form an expression of the knowledge of God, and as God is eternal, His knowledge, the *Veda*, too is eternal. (2) They all accept the cyclic theory of creation. The whole of creation appears and disappears in a repetitive cyclic process. They postulate two factors as basic to creation—akasha which is something like ether and prana the cosmic energy. By the vibrations of prana in the material akasha, the emergence and subsidence of the cosmos take place in the cyclic order. The doctrine of karma, the idea of God, the ideal of salvation (moksha) are some of the other common points, though there are great differences in their interpretation.

42.3 THE DUALISTIC SCHOOL

Regarding the Vedantic schools, there are three important ones among these to be considered. Taking the dualistic schools first, they accept God, souls and nature as three distinct entities, eternally existing in their separation. (It will be relevant to supplement this statement by adding that while in the earlier non-Vedantic dualisms, all these were independent entities, the Vedantic dualism holds that God alone is an independent entity, while the others are absolutely dependent upon Him.) God manifests the universe and rules over it. Nature and souls are involved in this manifestation and they undergo change, but God is unchanging. God is personal in that He has an infinite number of blessed qualities and attributes, in that He is approachable and responsive, in that He can be prayed to and adored, and in that He is responsive to such prayer and love. God requires material to work with, and nature (*prakriti*) is that material. Some pre-Vedantic dualists held that this ultimate stuff of creation consists of an infinite number of minute indivisible atoms, but Vedantic dualism holds that it is indiscrete and undifferentiated matter (*prakriti*) and it is out of it that God projects the universe. They conceive God as devoid of all evil qualities and make Him the centre of all blessed attributes.

Now the firs difficulty about a dualistic God is the question: How there happens to be so much of evil in the creation of a God who has only blessed attributes and who is full of love and mercy? Unlike some other religions, the Vedanta did not discover a Satan to account for the presence of evil. They put the blame exclusively on man.

It has been possible for Vedantic dualists to do so, because they do not accept that souls and matter were created at a given time out of nothing. As there is no absolute beginning, we can think of the soul as coming with endowments gained in past births. Today we work with whatever endowments we have acquired in the past, and by our present work we determine our fate for tomorrow. Thus if we ourselves are shaping our destiny for the future, it is logical to hold that our present has been shaped by what we have done in the past. As creation is without a beginning in time, we have to accept that we have had countless embodiments in the past, and thus we have been always shaping our future, whether it be characterised by happiness or misery, by our own actions. So the present suffering of society is due to the past wickedness of man. God is not to blame. He is the eternally merciful Father. We reap what we sow.

Another idea of dualistic Vedanta is that every soul must eventually attain salvation. Salvation means getting out of the eternal cycle of births and deaths, in which the *jiva* acquires karma and reaps its fruits through experiences that give pleasure and pain. To undergo the mixed experience of pleasure and pain, they come to the earth sphere, and when they are entitled for felicities of a higher order, they are embodied in the worlds of the devas or swarga (heavens). But these heavens and even the positions of deities presiding over them are temporary. They are acquired through good karma whose effects are temporal, and when the meritorious karma to one's credit is exhausted by enjoyment, the *jiva* comes for embodiment again to the earth sphere to acquire new karma. But according to dualism, beyond these temporary heavens there is the supreme abode of the divine person which cannot be attained as a result of any action, but only through pure devotion and dedication of all one's thoughts and deeds to Him. On such devotees His grace is bestowed, and by that they are lifted from the cycle of births and deaths, and restored to the supreme abode. The divine abode is known by several names as *Satyaloka*, Vaikuntha, Kailasa, etc. There is no more downfall for souls that attain to this supreme abode. They are forever in spiritual bliss in the presence of the divine person.

These dualists declare that man's tenacious hold on 'me and mine' is the cause of all trouble, of all bondage in samsara. According to them to think of one's property and one's family as 'mine' is wrong. They all belong to God, and one is only God's caretaker for the time being. The dualists are great vegetarians, and if they are asked why animals should not be killed for food, they will say, 'Because it is the Lord's'. Thus when a man has come to a state in which he is devoid of 'me and mine', when he has abandoned everything of his to the Lord, when he could do everything only for the pleasure of the Lord and not for any reward, then his heart will get purified and will come to love the Lord without any extraneous motives. The Lord is all attractiveness, but so long as the soul is covered with a thick coating of selfishness and thinks of worldly enjoyment, it cannot feel that attraction, as an iron piece covered with a thick coat of mud cannot feel the pull of a magnet. But the Lord's attraction becomes spontaneous when the soul is purified. These persons endowed with pure and unmotivated love will never pray to God for any material gift. If they are in need of these minor worldly felicities, they may adore the various minor deities or perform appropriate rituals. The Supreme Being should be approached only for salvation, abandoning all idea of 'me and mine' and desire for worldly gratification.

42.3 QUALIFIED NON-DUALISM

While the dualistic standpoint is reflected in the *Upanishads* also, the trend of their teaching is mainly

towards unity. In dualism this is very little in evidence
except in the idea that God is the only independent entity and matter and souls have only existence dependent on Him. It is in qualified non-dualism that Vedanta
in the sense of a quest after the unity of all existence
begins. These Vedantists start by making the statement
that the effect is never different from the cause, but only
the cause reproduced in another form. If the universe
is the effect and God its cause, they must be identical.
But this identity according to them is an identity in
difference. God, soul and nature are three entities, but
they are inseparably related as one organic whole, just
as the limbs and the body and the soul of an organism
constitute one entity in spite of their distinctiveness.
God is the soul of the universe, while souls and nature,
His inseparable attributes, constitute His body or limbs.
As the body of God, they are one with Him. Here no
question of the finite limiting the Infinite arises, because
the finite itself is a constitutive factor in the totality of
the Infinite. The *jiva's* spiritual consciousness contracts
in the state of ignorance and expands in liberation.
Prakriti also contracts and expands. Its expansion is the
projection of the universe into the manifested or effect
state. Its contraction is *pralaya* or dissolution. This process goes on eternally like night and day. The creative
state gives opportunity for *jivas* to enjoy the fruits of
the karma in repeated embodiments, gain experience

and ultimately be blessed with divine love and thereby attain salvation.

It is a doctrine of unity in so far as matter and souls form inseparably one with God as His body or His qualification. God is thus both the material and efficient cause of the universe, unlike in pure dualism. Being the body of God, matter and souls are one with Him, and for this reason it can be said that it is God, the cause of all causes, who has become the world. But at the same time the change that takes place in the manifestation as the world, does not affect Him, because He is only its soul.

All souls are in their essential nature pure and en-dowed with Self-consciousness. But by evil karma the powers of the soul shrink. In liberation consciousness expands. The souls are countless and are compared to sparks coming from a fire.

The God of the qualified non-dualist is a personal God endowed with innumerable auspicious qualities. But He is also everywhere as the indwelling spirit. He is not only the soul of the universe as a whole, but is in-dwelling every atom constituting it. Thus when it is said that God is the universe, or a part of the universe like the neighbouring wall is God, it is not meant that He has become the wall, ceasing to be His Self, as material objects have to do in such transformations, but that He is already in the wall, which being a part of universal matter (*prakriti*), constitutes His body.

42.4 ADVAITISM

The third strand of thought, Advaitism, is the fairest flower of the Upanishadic thought and the noblest philosophy that the human mind has conceived in any part of the world. But as the ordinary human mind always wants to lean on somebody's help, this doctrine which inculcates reliance on one's own Self, is difficult for many to understand and to practise. Generally people want a comfortable religion, not the truth. Advaitism is for the few who dare to conceive the truth, who dare to take it and who dare to follow it to the end.

'What does the Advaitist declare? He says, if there is a God, that God must be both the material and the efficient cause of the universe. Not only is He the creator, but He is also the created.' But then how can God, the pure spirit, become the universe which is dull and inert, unless He loses his own essential nature? The answer is that it is only apparently so. That which all ignorant people see as the universe, does not really exist. The view of the ignorant man is mere self-hypnotism. There is but one existence, the Infinite and the ever-blessed One. In that existence we dream all these various dreams. Seen through the senses, it appears as matter, through the intellect as souls, and through the spirit as God. To the man who throws upon himself the veils which the world calls wickedness and evil, this very universe will change and become a hideous place. To another man who wants enjoyments, this very universe will change its appearance and become a heaven; and to the perfect man the whole thing will vanish and will become his own Self.

'Everyone and everything is the Atman—the Self—the sexless, the pure, the ever-blessed. It is the name, the form, the body, which are material, and they make all this difference. If you take away these two differences of name and form, the whole universe is one; there are no two, but one everywhere. You and I are one. ... All these heavens, all these earths, and all these places are vain imaginations of the mind. They do not exist, never existed in the past, and never will exist in the future.'

There is but one Soul in the universe, not two. It neither comes nor goes. It is neither born, nor dies, nor reincarnates. 'I am omnipotent, eternal. Where can I go? Where am I not already? I am reading this book of nature. Page after page I am finishing and turning over, and one dream of life after another goes away.'

'What does the Advaitist preach? He dethrones all the gods that ever existed, or ever will exist in the universe and places on that throne the Self of man, the Atman, higher than the sun and the moon, higher than the heavens, greater than this great universe itself. ... I am to worship, therefore, none but myself. "I worship my Self," says the Advaitist. To whom shall I bow down? I salute my Self. To whom shall I go for help? Who can help me, the Infinite Being of the universe? These are foolish dreams, hallucinations. ...' When the dualist weeps and cries for help from some being in the skies 'and the help comes. ... but it comes from within himself' ; for the sky and the being he thought of as residing there, are really within himself. Only ignorance hides this truth from him. 'Thus man, after this vain search after various gods outside himself, completes the circle, and comes back to the point from which he started—the human soul, and he finds that the God whom he was searching in hill and dale, whom he was seeking in every brook, in every temple, in churches and heavens, that God whom he was even imagining as sitting in heaven and ruling the world, is his own Self. I am He and He is I. None but I was God, and this little I never existed.'

A question will be raised against this position. How did the perfect God get deluded? The answer is that He never was deluded. How could a perfect God have ever been dreaming? The very question is absurd. Illusion arises from illusion alone. There will be no illusion as soon as the truth is seen. Illusion never rests on God, the Truth, the Atman. You are never in illusion, it is illusion that is in you, before you. As before the eternal blue sky, clouds of various hues and colours come, remain for a short time and disappear, leaving it as blue as ever, even so are you the eternally pure, the eternally perfect.

These are the salient points of the three steps which Indian religious thought has taken in regard to God. It went from the external God to the internal cosmic person, God immanent in the universe, and ended in identifying the soul itself with God, and that God, with whom this soul is one, as the basis of this manifestation as the universe. As society exists today, all these stages are necessary to suit the needs of men at different stages of evolution. The three steps do not contradict one another. Each succeeding one is the fulfilment of the earlier one. Each man has to be taken where he stands and given a helping hand to go forward. Such is the method of the Vedantic teachers.

43

THE ATMAN—ITS BONDAGE AND FREEDOM

43.1 THE SPIRITUAL ESSENCE IN MAN

The Advaita philosophy accepts Brahman, the Absolute Being, as the only Reality. All the multiplicity experienced is only an apparent manifestation of that Reality. The multiplicity, though experienced, is not actually there, since the Absolute Brahman never changes actually into the multiplicity. It is *mithya*, an apparent manifestation only. The power of apparent manifestation is called maya. Each embodied being is in reality that Brahman, but due to maya, He appears as a body-mind. Minus this maya, the *jiva* is Brahman. Brahman with reference to the body is also called Atman, the spiritual essence.

According to this philosophy, a *jiva*, an embodied being, has three strands in him. At the core he is the Atman; he has an internal coating which is mental, and an external coating which is physical.

The Atman, the spiritual essence in man, is immaterial and immortal, being Brahman Himself. Not being a compound, it cannot disintegrate or perish. For the same reason it is eternal, without a beginning. Just as it is not conditioned by time, it is not conditioned by space also. It is, therefore, all-pervading. The Atman in every one is the same, and it is simultaneously everywhere—in the sun, the moon or any part of the earth. But the Atman or the Self functions through the mind and the body. It is because of the presence of the Atman that the body-mind, in itself inert, is characterised by Self-consciousness.

The Atman, being one with Brahman, never comes and goes, is never born or dies. It is nature that is moving, super-imposing its movements on the spirit through its reflection in it. Identifying himself with the reflection, the Atman ignorantly thinks he is moving, while in fact it is nature only that is moving. When the Atman thinks this way, he is in bondage; but when he comes to discover that he never moves, that he is omnipresent, then he is free. The Atman in bondage is called the *jiva*. As *jiva*, the Atman is associated with the adjuncts of the subtle body, which is mental, and of the gross body, which is physical. The physical body perishes at death, but the subtle mental body, with all the tendencies, impressions, and moral and spiritual efficiencies gathered during a lifetime inhering in it, survives the physical body, and it transmigrates as other gross bodies on this earth sphere itself or in subtler regions according to the merits and demerits it has acquired in life. This transmigratory process continues until the embodied being, the *jiva*, realises his real nature as the Atman. Then the subtle body also perishes, and the *jiva* attains liberation by realising his unity with Brahman.

43.2 THE DOCTRINE OF KARMA AND REBIRTH

In discussing the embodied state of the Atman as the *jiva*, this doctrine of karma and rebirth is of fundamental importance. Akasa and prana, the two factors of nature, come together and manufacture new bodies according to the karmic tendencies of the individual. It can be illustrated by the examples of eddies of whirlwinds in the atmosphere. Different currents of air coming from different directions meet and at the meeting point, go on rotating. Into the rotating point, dust, paper, straw, etc., are drawn in and they form a whirling unit. Then they are dropped down as the current of wind transfers itself to another spot, to which materials are drawn from the neighbourhood. The whirl stops when the energies are exhausted. The repeated embodiments caused by the prana drawing materials according to the karmic tendencies, may be likened to this.

Again the transmigrating of the *jiva* may be compared to the course of a ball that is being hit with a mallet in a hall, causing it to strike different points until it flies out of the room. When and with what velocity it will fly out, will be determined by the forces that have been acting upon it in the room. In the same way, all our actions in this life will determine the course we take in the next, including the acquisition of the mental and physical equipments we shall be having at the next birth. Those products of karmic efficiencies present themselves naturally in the new individual.

Our present birth is thus the cumulative result of our actions in the past births. Each embodiment with birth and death as its two ends is like a link in a chain. With our knowledge of the general nature of our present link, we can know the general nature of the preceding and succeeding ones, and thus of the whole chain which extends up to a distance that cannot be determined. Thus the whole chain is a repetition of similar links, with internal differences of course, rounded with birth and death at the two ends.

43.3 *SAMSARA*

All the universe was (or has been) Brahman. The world has, as it were, been projected by Him, and has been moving on to go back ultimately to that source from which it was projected, just as the electricity which comes out of the dynamo completes the circuit and returns to it. The same is the case with the soul. Projected from Brahman it passes through all sorts of vegetable and animal forms, and at last it is in man. In the human body it gets an embodiment where it can make a conscious effort to reach the goal, the realisation of one's nature as Brahman. Without one's knowledge this struggle towards that goal is going on. All competitions and struggles in animal life and elsewhere, all social struggles and wars are but expressions of this eternal struggle to get back to that pristine state.

Some people have a horror to be told that the soul of man has had plant and animal life as antecedent conditions before attaining to humanity. They do not stop to think what will be the condition of the countless number of animals. They too have souls and are on the path of evolution to the highest destiny. But being mere creatures of instinct at their level of evolution, they can make no conscious effort to hasten their evolution. But at the human level, with the dawn of *buddhi*, the power of reflection and reasoning, man is given the choice of quickly putting an end to this eternally recurring repetitive process of life and death, which is called in Indian thought *samsara*.

As against this idea of freedom from *samsara*, some may argue there is no need of getting out of it. It is in itself enjoyable; and by the application of science and technology, it can be made still more enjoyable. It is true that the vast majority of people are satisfied with the life of the senses as it is constituted, and will go on with the enjoyments and sufferings of it, without caring much for the distant prospect of coming out of the round or getting out of it. The spiritual philosophy is addressed to people who have seen through the nature of the worldly life and do not see much worth in it as such, or who find even the struggle, pleasures and painful experiences of life meaningful only on the acceptance of this ultimate goal. Such persons will easily see that life can never be free from miseries and from the repetitiveness and determinism of nature, from which they long to escape. However much we may try to make this world perfect and whatever improvement we believe we are making, this world of ours is sure to be broken to pieces ultimately. The idea of making it perfect will easily be found to be a chimera, although limited improvements here and there by human endeavour may be possible in a relative sense.

Besides, we have been having these experiences in the world innumerable times. What we call now the world and the conditions prevailing in it, have occurred time without number in the course of nature's repetitive process. The law of chance tells us that when vast numbers of things are shaken innumerable times, the same combinations will be occurring time and again in the course of vast stretches of time. In the same way, however distant may be the period, the same combinations and dissolutions will happen again and again, and the same birth, eating, drinking, mating, and death will come round again and again. Every form, beginning from the little worm and ending in man, is like one of the cars of the Chicago Ferris wheel. It is in motion all the time, but the occupants change. A man goes into a car, moves with the wheel and comes out. The wheel goes on and on. A soul enters one form, resides in it for a time, then leaves it, and goes into another and quits that again for a third. Thus the soul goes on, till it comes out of the wheel and becomes free.

At the lower levels of life, they cannot get free. But man, if he is tired of this meaningless process and the little joys and sufferings incidental to it, has the choice to extricate himself from it and gain that spiritual state which is the source of everything.

44

THE REAL AND THE APPARENT MAN

Just as man wants to know about the external world, he wants also to know about himself and his destiny. Hence he has developed natural sciences and philosophy. The Vedanta which represents the best effort of the Indian mind in this direction, is a quest after the unity of existence, and the question is raised what is that by knowing which everything can be known. Hindu philosophers have reduced the whole objective universe into one stuff, the akasha, and all kinds of forces working in it into one basic energy, the prana. Prana acting on the akasha is creating the whole of this universe. In the beginning of a cycle this prana sleeps as it were, in the infinite ocean of akasha. Motionless, it existed. Then as the prana begins to vibrate, out of this ocean of akasha comes out in stages the various worlds, gross and subtle, the celestial systems, our own earth with its human beings, animals, plants, etc., as also the manifestation of all forms of force known to us as gravitation, radiation, electricity, heat, etc. Every manifestation of force is that of prana, and every material manifestation, of akasha. This in brief is the evolution of the cosmos.

The creative process is in cycles—a period of evolution or manifestation followed by one of dissolution or involution. At the end of the cycle of manifestation, all gross things dissolve into their finer states—solids into liquids, liquids into gases, gases into heat vibrations, and that finally into akasha, and all forces into prana. Then the prana is 'asleep' without vibrations for a long period, equal to the period of manifestation, and afterwards the new cycle begins once more, the prana starting to vibrate again.

The cosmic process up to this is largely in line with modern scientific conceptions. But the discovery of unity is still far off. The Indian thinkers therefore unify akasha and prana as a twofold manifestation of a still finer entity—the mahat or universal mind. It is out of the universal thought that matter and energy emerged.

44.2 SOUL AS THE PRINCIPLE OF UNITY IN MAN

The quest after unity has also to be followed from the point of view of psychology. Let us analyse what happens when man experiences sensations. First the eye, the instrument of sight, comes into contact with the light rays carrying the image of the object etc. Behind the eye is the organ of vision in the brain centre. If it is removed, the eye by itself can give no vision. Even this is not sufficient. The mind must be attached to the organ if we are to see. For example, if we are hearing delightful music intently, we will fail to notice things before our eyes. It is only when the mind attaches itself to the organ that the latter can function. The mind can sort out and determine the nature of the present impressions only in comparison with all the past. But before it becomes a perception, a reaction from a Self-conscious substratum as 'I see', has also got to come. This comes only when the impressions receive the recognition of the soul of man, the only entity in man that is Self-conscious and can give the experience 'I see' to the sensations that are brought to it by the mechanism of perception. Besides, the physical and mental sheaths of man are continuously changing. There must be a stable background on which the flow of sensations have to be registered, as when a film is shown, a stable screen is required for the formation of the images projected. Without that screen no image will be found. So the idea that there must be a Self-conscious and stable background for sensations to take a Self-conscious form, a soul, an essence, an intelligent spirit distinct from nature's changing phenomena—has to be accepted.

The analogy of the human personality is extended by many philosophers to the understanding of the cosmos also. It has already been said that it is the cosmic mind that splits into akasha and prana and forms the universe. Behind the cosmic mind is the universal spirit, which in ordinary parlance we call God. Thus the whole of nature and the living beings included in it, form, as it were, the body of God according to some philosophers. Can't this idea be extended to man also, and may we not say that the spirit and the body form a unity? Here we come to the question of the nature of the unity that exists between God and souls and matter, as also the different strata in man. The views of Vedantic schools on these questions differ.

44.3 DUALISM

According to dualism, the soul of man is an immortal spiritual entity. Mortality is dissolution into parts, but the spirit is not such a combination. It is a simple. For the same reason it has existed eternally too, and it will pass from the present span of life to others till it is liberated. When the body dies, the vital functions of the man go back to his mind, the mind gets dissolved in prana, and the prana enters into the soul of man. The soul, clothed in a subtle body, in which all the tendencies, good and bad, acquired in the past are latent, passes out of the body. The destiny of the soul in the hereafter is determined by the tendencies, merits and demerits, he has acquired by his actions in life and are conveyed through the subtle body.

There are three goals for the departing soul according to their spiritual evolution and moral acquisitions in the past. The most spiritual persons who have devoted their life to worship of God and dedicated service go along the bright path to *Brahmaloka*, guided by a blessed divine messenger. In the *Brahmaloka* their devotion and knowledge reach perfection, and at the time of cosmic dissolution they get merged in Brahman. According to the dualistic schools like those of the *Vaishnavas*, who maintain that the soul is by nature different from God and will remain distinct even in salvation, the *jivas* clothed in the divine spiritual body live for eternity in *Vaikuntha*, an eternal sphere of *Brahmaloka*, serving Narayana who is manifest to them as the divine person.

The lesser type of men who are activated by selfish desires and have been performing ritualistic works and charitable actions with rewards in view, go by the path of smoke, to the paradise (*Swarga-loka*) and there enjoy such of the felicities of that sphere as they are eligible to by their meritorious works. At the exhaustion of their merits, they come back to the earth with their residuary karmic efficiencies and are born as men in appropriate bodies for further enjoyments and sufferings and the acquisition of new karma, or if they choose, for the pursuit of the path to spiritual perfection. Wicked men become ghosts and demons, and after they have suffered in those states for their misdeeds, they may get embodiments as animals also. Ultimately they become men again, and get another chance to attain spiritual progress. Now it is believed that none of these spheres and forms of life—*Brahmaloka* or paradise, the nether regions or the animal bodies—offer scope to the *jivas* to acquire new karma. They enjoy or suffer for their past karmas in such embodiments, and they have to be born as men again to acquire new karmic efficiency for enjoyments in heaven or for striving for liberation. This is the special merit of human birth and people are therefore exhorted not to neglect or misuse that opportunity. Of the higher spheres, *Brahmaloka* alone offers the environment for higher spiritual evolution, and that sphere is attained only by great spiritual striving in earthly life.

44.4 BUDDHIST CRITICISM OF DUALISTIC THEORY

Now the soul theory, namely, that behind the changing body-mind phenomenon there must necessarily be a changeless substratum, has been criticised by the Buddhist thinkers as an unnecessary assumption. It is unnecessarily bringing in an extraneous factor. Nature is a self-sufficient and self-explaining entity. A lighted torch circling very fast can produce an illusory appearance of a circle of light, though there is no actual circle but only points of light. So also the sense of unity behind the fast changing body and mind is an illusory perception, and no permanent soul, external to them, need be invoked to explain this sense. Everything is an aggregate of qualities; there is no need for a hypothetical substance for them to inhere in. These Buddhist criticism of the soul theory has much in common with modern scientific and philosophic thinking.

44.5 ADVAITIC RECONCILIATION

The dualist's contention that we can understand change only with reference to a changeless background is correct. But when he says that this background is something entirely different from the body and mind, he is not correct. In the same way when the Buddhist says that the whole universe is a mass of change, he is perfectly right; for, so long as I consider myself separate from the universe, stand back and look at the body, mind and the world as something before me, so long as there are two entities, the observer and the thing observed, it will appear always that the universe is a mass of change. But the Reality is that there is both change and changelessness in experience. It is not that the soul and the mind and the body are three separate existences; for, the organism made of these three is really one. But it is not at the same time all these. He who sees the body, does not see the mind even; he who sees the mind, does not see what he calls the soul; and he who sees the soul—for him the body and the mind have vanished. He who sees only motion never sees absolute calm, and he who sees absolute calm—for him motion has vanished. A rope is taken for a snake. He who sees the rope as the snake, for him the rope has vanished, but when the delusion ceases and he looks at the rope, the snake has vanished.

'There is then but one all-comprehending existence, and that one appears as manifold. This Self or Soul or Substance is all that exists in the universe. That Self or Substance or Soul is, in the language of non-dualism, the Brahman. ...' It is like the boisterous waves on the surface of the sea and its calm substratum. Who can make a difference between the sea and its wavy surface? The wave is but a name and a form, and it will vanish when the disturbance subsides. The wave is entirely dependent on the sea, but not the sea on the existence of the waves.

The idea of duality or two is entirely false, and the whole universe, as we ordinarily know it, is the result of this false knowledge. 'When discrimination comes and man finds there are not two but one, he finds that he is himself this universe. ... There is, therefore, but one Atman, one Self, eternally pure, eternally perfect, unchangeable, unchanged; it has never changed; ar d

all these various changes in the universe are but appearances in that one Self.' These appearances, resulting from
'name and form is the outcome of what is called Maya.
It is this Maya that is making individuals, making one
appear different from another. Yet it has no existence.
Maya cannot be said to exist' for, the names and the
forms it gives rise to, cannot be said to exist, because
they depend on the existence of a substratum. It cannot,
however be said not to exist either, because it gives us the
experience of all these diversities, however transitorily.
So the presentations of maya are called appearances,
which give one the idea of entities that are not actually
there but are none-the-less experienced. It is out of the
one Infinite existence that maya is showing this manifold universe of appearances. In substance it is all one.

This oneness of all existence is being proved at a
material level even by modern science. It has been demonstrated 'that you and I, the sun, the moon, and the
stars are but the different names of different spots in the
same ocean of matter, and that this matter is continuously changing in its configuration. ... all these names
are fictitious; they have no reality, because the whole
is a continuously changing mass of matter. This very
same universe, from another standpoint, is an ocean
of thought, where each one of us is a point called a
particular mind. You are a mind, I am a mind, everyone is a mind; and the very same universe viewed from

the standpoint of knowledge, when the eyes have been
cleared of delusions, when the mind has become pure,
appears to be the unbroken Absolute Being, the ever
pure, the unchangeable, the immortal.'

44.6 THE ADVAITIC EXPLANATION OF ESCHATOLOGY

In the light of the Advaitic doctrine, what becomes
of the threefold eschatology of the dualists? Advaita
maintains that the Self of man, being omnipresent and
ever-free, the ideas of it being born, dying, going to
different spheres, etc., are all 'childish dream and pu-
erile illusion', and that they 'vanish immediately for the
perfect. For the nearly perfect it vanishes after showing
them the several scenes up to Brahmaloka. It continues
for the ignorant'

These experiences of life here and hereafter are comparable to a man studying a book. Page after page is
being turned. But who changes, not the man but the
book. The whole of nature is a book before the soul,
and chapter after chapter is being turned over. When
one page is over, a fresh one comes, but the soul never
changes. Birth and death are in nature, not in the spirit.
Yet the ignorant are deluded and attribute it to the Self,
just as ignorant men think the sun is moving and not
the earth.

When men are in a certain frame of mind, they see

this one existence as earth, as the sun, moon, stars, etc., and all who are in the same frame of mind see them too. 'Between you and me there may be millions of beings on different planes of existence. They will never see us, nor we them; we only see those who are in the same state of mind and on the same plane with us. Those musical instruments respond which have the same attunement of vibration, as it were; if the state of vibration, which they call "man-vibration", should be changed, no longer would men be seen here; the whole "man-universe" would vanish, and instead of that, other scenery would come before us, perhaps gods and the god-universe, or perhaps, for the wicked man, devils and the diabolic world; but all would be only different views of the one universe. ... Those who have been dreaming of going to a God who is sitting on a throne, and of standing there praising Him all their lives, when they die, will simply see a vision of what they have in their minds; this very universe will simply change into a vast heaven, with all sorts of winged beings flying about and a God sitting on a throne. These heavens are all of man's own making. So what the dualist says is true, says the Advaitin, but it is all simply of his own making. These spheres and devils and gods and re-incarnations and transmigrations are all mythology; so also is this human life. The great mistake that men always make is to think that this life alone is true. They understand it well enough when other things are called mythologies, but are never willing to admit the same of their own position.'

'It is the greatest of all lies that we are mere men; we are the God of the universe. In worshipping God we have been always worshipping our own hidden Self.' When 'the real nature of man now stands unfolded to him as being higher than heaven, more perfect than this universe of ours, more infinite than infinite time, more omnipresent than the omnipresent ether. ... For that man disappears the whole universe, as it were.' It 'becomes transfigured into one infinite, unbreakable, unchangeable existence, and the knowing man finds that he is one with that existence. ... The real man is the one Unit Existence'. 'He is the whole universe. Either say he is the whole universe or say that to him there is no universe. ... It is a lie to say that I am a man or a woman, or to say that I belong to this country or that. All the world is my country, the whole universe is mine, because I have clothed myself with it as my body.' all

44.7 ADVAITA: ITS RELEVANCE TO ETHICS AND UTILITY

There are people in this world who assert this doctrine, and at the same time lead an evil life. When questioned about it, they reply that these are the delusions of their critics and that they themselves are doing nothing. This is rank hypocrisy. That both evil and good are conditioned manifestations of the soul is true, but it is also true that evil is the most external coating and the good the nearest one to the real man, the Self. Unless the man has cut through the layers of evil, he cannot reach the layer of good, and unless he has passed through both the layers of good and evil, he cannot reach the Self. So whatever actions are done by a man established in the sense of unity on account of residuary karma, will be ethically sublime and beneficial to the world. They can do no evil. Those whose behaviour is to the contrary, are mere talkers. Realisation is different from talking. The realised man takes no false steps, nor is he shaken from his conviction by all criticism, just as a man who has actually gone to a country only laughs at others who question the existence of that country.

The man who has attained to this knowledge of reality is called the 'Living Free', the jivan-mukta or one liberated in this life itself. His condition is like that of a man travelling in a desert, who first saw a mirage there and went to take water from it, but after having realised the nature of the illusory nature of the spectacle before him, continued to walk, seeing the mirage all the time but not deluded as before. Residual karma keeps up his body until it is exhausted. But that karma will only be of a beneficial nature, and no evil can come out of him. On the other hand such people alone can do real good to others.

An allied question that is asked is about the utility of such a realisation for the world at large. First of all the question is absurd, being based on this three days wonder that we call the world. It is comparable in its silliness to the question of a child about an important finding of scientific research, Does it bring gingerbread? Apart from this, it is also of the highest utility. There are some who mistakenly think that it will dry up all springs of love in the human heart. The fact, however, is just the opposite. So long as you have a self-centred outlook on men and things, you can have no real love. Love of a self-centred man will only be high-sounding selfishness. Those who thought least of their own individualities have always been the greatest workers for the good of the world. World-movers have come from the ranks of those in whom the little self is dead and God stands in its place. There is nothing like the knowledge of the unity of all existence that can generate universal love and make dull the edge of heartless competition and selfish struggle that have reduced the world to a state of misery. If there are a number of such men of realisation in the world, everything in society will be changed and transfigured. 'No more will you stand up and sneeringly cast a glance at a poor man or woman who has made a mistake. No more, ladies, will you look

down with contempt upon the poor woman who walks
the street in the night, because you will see even there
God Himself. No more will you think of jealousy and
punishments. They will all vanish; and love, the great
ideal of love, will be so powerful that no whip and cord
will be necessary to guide mankind aright.'